DARIO
America's Gift to an Immigrant

To Joe and Clarke.
All God's Blessings.

Dario Antonini

xulon PRESS

America's Gift to an Immigrant
by Dario Antonucci

Printed in the United States of America

ISBN 9781619046276

Bible Quotation: 1 Corinthians 15:10

New International Version (NIV)

10 But by the grace of God I am what I am, and his grace to me was not without effect. No, I worked harder than all of them—yet not I, but the grace of God that was with me.

www.xulonpress.com

DARIO

An Autobiography

Immigrant, USA WWII Veteran, Engineer,
Husband, Father and Grandfather

ACKNOWLEDGEMENTS

In order to accomplish this manuscript it is only right that I recognize with deep appreciation and thanks the members of my family whose help has made this document possible.

My granddaughter Emily Calvert who did all the typing and some formatting, my daughter Daria for formatting and scanning all the pictures and doing the computer operations in transmitting the text and pictures to the publisher; and my daughter Rosemary and son-in-law Mark Calvert for scanning the typed text into the computer and rescuing me when I got into trouble with the computer operations.

Annette 'Little Nettie' and Dario

Forward

I hope you will read this biography of an extraordinary ancestor carefully. Dad, Grandpa, Dario is a very caring, honest, intelligent, hard working, good human being. Dario is the love of my life now and forever.

Our life together was exceptional! He did what no other man could do for me. He has taken me to the home of my ancestors in Italy; he has taken me where he served in WWII, India, Burma where we were honored. He has taken me to China twice, where we were greeted like very important people, and made to feel very special, We flew over the "Hump"- the Himalayas; the very same extraordinary route used during WWII to deliver troops and supplies used to fight the Japanese forces.

We believe we were very good children towards our parents, and we were very good parents to our children. God watched over us throughout our lives.

Our lives together were guided by the rules: our children first, our parents second and our marriage third. If we had to live over again, we would do the same thing except we would try to spend more time alone together if possible.

It was only after we moved to Tennessee that we have had more time to devote to each other and to get to know each other fully.

Again, I ask you to read this biography carefully. " You cannot know where you are going if you don't know where you came from". May God bless you and watch over you.

> With Love,
> Wife, Mother and Grandmother
> Annette Antonucci

How it All Began

S t. Marco Argentano, Province of Cosenza in the Italian Region of Calabria, lived the families of Guerci and Lecce. The Guerci family lived in the district of Spinetto and the Lecce family lived in the district of Stamile. It was and still is an area of small and medium means struggling farmers, where all farming is done mostly manually because of the hilly formation of the land.

The homes during the 1800's and up to World War II, in this area, were built of mud and straw bricks or blocks. There were paths but no roads.

Sometime in early 1915 a marriage was being arranged, through a marriage maker, (Masciata), between the family of Giuseppe and Maddalene Lecce and the family of Guerci. The designated bride Rosa Lecce and designated groom Emilio Guerci. The marriage took place in 1916, the bride Rosa Lecce and the groom Emilio Guerci. The honeymoon during those days was that the married couple would stay in their home for one week, to receive friends and well wishers bringing gifts and food. After the week was over everybody would go back to their work and toil.

Unfortunately, Emilio was called by the army to fight in World War I, 16 days after his marriage to Rosa. Three weeks after he reported for duty he was killed in the battle of Caporetto, Trieste (then part of Italy). The young bride became a widow at the age of 20 years.

During this same period a young man of 19 years was called to duty to fight in WWI for Italy, in the same battle of Caporetto,

Trieste. He survived the battle but was captured and made a prisoner of war by the Austrians in late 1917.

The Austrians treated their prisoners of war very badly. They were mistreated like animals, and abandoned in the cold and rain. Many of the prisoners died from starvation, sickness and frozen to death. The young man, Angelo Antonucci, that was called to duty about the same time as Emilio Guerci, was rescued and liberated by the Allies early in 1918, and carried away, too weak from starvation and sick to walk. He was sent to a hospital and recovered.

As soon as this soldier, Angelo Antonucci, got his health back, he was sent to Tripoli, called Tripolitania, Libya, then an Italian possession. He served there in 1919 and early 1920, when he was returned to Italy. He was discharged from the Italian Army in May 1920.

Angelo Antonucci, my father to be, was born, as with his five brothers and three sisters, in St. Marco Argentano, Province of Cosenza; in a family district called Richietto, located in a valley below the Cathedral Viscovato (presently still an active cathedral).

His parents were tenant farmers, but as the boys grew none of them were inclined to stay there except Angelo, who was the youngest of the brothers. Upon him fell the burden of farming and helping his youngest sister and mother, since his father, Gaetano, died when Angelo was very young. My grandmother and Aunt and Angelo all worked in the fields to survive.

At about the age of 16, Angelo, his mother Giuseppina and his young sister Emilia decided to look for a homestead and move away from the town. Angelo's oldest sisters were already married when he went to fight in the war, Pasqualina around 1902-3, and Rosina right after.

They found a homestead about six acres, eight or nine kilometers south of St. Marco Argentano, in a district called Iotta. This would have been around 1913, whereby Angelo would have been 16 years old.

They managed to build a two room mud brick house on the highest point of the hilly terrain, overlooking very deep valleys on the north and south. One room was for mother and daughter, and the other for Angelo, the son. The rooms were not internally connected, had separate outside doors. Each room had the outside door and two windows each, with no glass—just handmade shutters, and dirt floors. The ceilings were the terra cotta tiles (ceramila) that were also the roof, no attics. One corner of each room was for fire and cooking.

In 1920, after Angelo was discharged from the army, a marriage arrangement was being worked out between Angelo Antonucci and the widow Rosa Lecce. There was, however, one problem—Angelo, by tradition, could not get married until his young sister was married first. His sister Emilia could not get married until she had a dowry. Her mother and brother, just out of the army, could not afford to give a dowry. This was relayed to Rosa and her parents.

Rosa, after her first husband was killed, received a small pension for his death from the government. Through an intermediary the suggestion was made to Rosa's parents that if they would help with Angelo's sister's dowry, Angelo's family would sign over the homestead to Rosa, from his mother and sister. I used to hear that Angelo and Rosa really loved each other and wanted to get married. So an agreement was reached—Rosa and her family helped with Emilia's dowry, and the homestead was in Rosa's name. Angelo and Rosa were married April 19, 1921. Rosa Lecce and Angelo Antonucci would become my mother and father.

After the wedding my father and mother lived in my grandmother's homestead.

My maternal grandparents were Giuseppe and Maddalena Lecce. They were both of Albanian (Albanese) descent some three or four generations back, and still spoke with a heavy Albanian accent, since they all formed their individual towns when they arrived in Italy. This would make the 6th partial Albanian generation for me.

My paternal grandparents were Giuseppina and Gaetano Antonucci. I never knew my grandfather since he died many years before I was born. My grandmother Giuseppina lived with us until her death in 1932.

It was a hard life. The land was mostly steep hills, and had to be worked by hand, mostly heavy hoes, picks, ad axes; men and women working side by side. My father had managed to acquire a team of oxen, and that helped in tilling and working some of the least hilly part of the land, but it was nonetheless a struggle.

On June 2, 1922 my sister Giulia was born; delivered by my two grandmothers. Just about this time my father applied to come to America on the quota system. In the meantime working his land, he managed to acquire another piece of land some three kilometers away, near water and able to be irrigated, called "Chiararia." This land had olives, trees, some oak trees and was level. Oak trees were an asset, since they were a main supply of acorns to feed and fatten hogs. This piece of land was also neighboring my Aunt Pascualina and her husband Francesco Caruso. Aunt Pasqualina being my father's oldest sister. They were two wonderful people, and a great help to my mother.

Early in August 1923, my father was notified that he was selected to emigrate to America on the quota program. He reported to a depot near Napoli (Naples) called Battipaglia (means: threshing hay), a major railroad depot in Italy. When he arrived, he met several other Italian men also selected through the quota program, going to America. From this depot all were escorted together by train to the dock in Naples, where they departed for America, stopping at Genoa to pick up additional passengers. These to –be immigrants traveled steerage (bottom of the ship) since none could afford anything better.

Toward the last week of August 1923, the ship docked in New York, and after going through Ellis Island, my father was met by his brother Ciccillo, who was living in Brooklyn, NY. Because my father had a place to go in America, he didn't have much trouble going through the customs and inspectors.

As soon as he got off the boat, my father looked for work—manual work—because that was all he knew how to do. He took jobs as a helper in construction work, subway construction, and the like. As soon as he settled down, he enrolled in night adult school to learn the English language. His Italian education was very minimal and limited, and mostly self-taught. All the while writing home to my mother, and sending what little money he made. My mother was keeping up the farm—working the soil, harvesting olives and figs, and everything else. Meanwhile she was pregnant with me.

The main crop in the farms in Southern Italy are grains such as wheat (mostly), barley, oats, etc. The seeding is done in November and the wheat fields are ready for weeding between the end of February and mid April- which is also the rainy season. The women and men go in wheat fields with small hoes and try to cut and eliminate all, or at least most, the damaging weeds- most of the time while it's raining. All the farmers usually help one another during this period, and also during harvest time.

It was the beginning of March 1924, and my mother was nine months pregnant, but just the same she was working in the fields weeding with my paternal grandmother (Nonna Giuseppina). On Friday, March 7, 1924, after working in the fields all day, she let my paternal grandmother know that she felt like she was going to be ready to deliver soon. The next day they, my mother and Grandmother, went again in the fields- but returned home in the early afternoon, my mother realizing that she was about to give birth.

My paternal Grandmother, Giuseppina, decided to send word to my maternal Grandmother, Maddalena, to come and assist. During these times there were no telephones, no roads and no means of communication except by voice and/or foot over the hills and valleys, very muddy at this time of year. Voice carried far and loud in this type of terrain. Therefore my paternal Grandmother yelled to the people living on the next hill across the valley. They heard the message, and repeated it over the next hill, until the message got to my maternal grandmother three to four kilometers away. That evening, Saturday March 8, my maternal grandmother arrived to the side of my mother, by foot and in the rain- over hills and valleys. My mother had begun labor.

The next morning Sunday, March 9, at 4:30 in the morning, the closest neighbor one half kilometer away, heard two gun shots from a pair of old dueling pistols that my grandmother fired. The neighbor knew that a boy was born to Rosa, my mother. I was born.

Two hours later, my grandmothers heard one loud gunshot being fired by the neighbor, Francesco Sarpa, letting them know that a girl was born to his wife Rosina.

The weather was pouring rain by the barrel during this time and three days thereafter. Next morning one of my grandmothers went to visit the neighbors' baby girl, and the neighbor, Francesco, came to visit the little boy- me. During this visit mother asked Francesco that if when he went to register his daughter in town if he also would register her son. He said he would as soon as the rain would slow down some, since he had to travel by foot the nine kilometers to the municipal building. That came on March 13, 1924; Francesco Sarpa came by my mother and asked "Rosa what name do you want for your son?" My mother told him to pick a good name for me. So the neighbor walked to town that morning and registered Dario Antonucci for me and Virgilia Sarpa for his daughter- March 13, 1924- that's why I am four days younger than my true age.

IOTTA:

So I was born, and that didn't mean that my mother was going to take a leave from the chores at hand. As soon as the heavy rain relented Mama was back weeding the wheat fields, while my paternal grandmother took care of her new grandson and 22 months granddaughter. Mama took a break every few hours to breast feed her new son, in the damp, cold one room home- with an open fire burning at one corner and usually filled with smoke.

During these days there were no such commodities as diapers, so babies were wrapped like mummy puppets- using a two to three meters long band, about three to four inches wide, made of linen or cotton cloth.

Meanwhile my father in the United States worked hard, long hours and sometimes in the worst working conditions- like most immigrants who came to this country to better themselves. Of course, they were taken advantage of because of their lack of education and deficiency in the English language. My father kept going to adult night school to learn the language, and looking for work where he could make a little more money to send home to help his family.

Near the end of the year that I was born he got a job working in a chandelier factory in Brooklyn, NY, an inside job. My father was a farmer all his life, outdoors, and this work was torture for him. So, in early 1925, he heard that a Paesane (countryman) from Italy had started a gardening-landscape business- mostly cutting grass, trimming hedges and general cleaning. He got on the train one day and traveled to Baldwin, Long Island to visit this gardener. This fellow turned out to have come from the same town of my father in Italy, and agreed to give my father a job doing general gardening. This man and his wife also ran a boarding house in Baldwin, and my father became one of their boarders.

Before my father left for America in 1923, he realized that my mother could not be able to handle the team of oxen and the plow to work the land. He asked his brother Vincent, some four or five years his senior, to take care of the oxen, with the condition he would help my mother in working the land.

This brother, Vincent, during the end of WWI had met and married this woman from Padua, Northern Italy. After they got married there was nothing my uncle could do aside from being a simple farmer. They returned to South Italy and his hometown. He was not a worker to begin with, but worked as a tenant farmer. So when my father charged him with the team of oxen, with the promise that his brother would use them to improve himself, instead he was convinced by his wife to sell the animals and go live in her home town of Padua.

The sale of the team of oxen was such a terrible blow to my mother that she became ill from it. Those animals represented such a huge amount to a farmer, and besides they were her husband's precious possession, and were to be used to help both my selfish uncle and my mother.

My mother, after my birth, had developed a case of pleurisy, which after the advent of my uncle disposing of my father's oxen, greatly aggravated her condition. Nevertheless, she kept working as usual in the fields and raising two children and, according to my grandmother, never complaining. Although both my grandmothers and my mother were illiterate, they were shrewd in business matters, and in running their farms. However, life was hard and somewhat primitive.

Growing Up

Growing up was a natural phenomena in Iotta. Once I reached six months I was liberated from the "fascia," that long strip of cloth that bundled babies to look like mummies, and immobilized every movement. Instead a dress was substituted so that I could move around and accompany my mother and grandmother in the fields. The day care consisted of the shade of an olive tree, oak tree, or similar conveniences. For comfort I was laid down on a sheet or old blanket spread on the ground. My baby sitter was my two year old sister, and was located always within visual and hearing distance of my mother working in the field nearby.

As we grew up our playground was the open fields, picking wild flowers, twigs, and little creatures like frogs, cicadas, and small lizards. As we grew older, climbing trees and stepping in mud puddles was always a popular sport.

When we reached three years old we were introduced to doing chores. My mother gave us very small baskets with handles, and we followed her in picking olives and acorns from the ground. I still vividly remember my bleeding knuckles. I would start complaining and sometimes crying to my mother, and she would kiss my "boo-boo," and tell me to try to pick some more if I could. She never forced us to do this chore, but we always did- following her example. She praised us and we were happy and felt good that we had helped, no matter how little. And that's how we grew up.

When I was six years old I was introduced to the feeding of chickens and hogs. We already were expert in collecting eggs and picking tomatoes and other items. We were already experts in picking blackberries. My sister was taught how to help my mother in the kitchen, starting fires and washing dishes and clothes. At six years or thereabouts I had learned how to ride a donkey bareback, and how to milk a goat. By the time I was seven I would ride the donkey to a roadside, government owned store to buy salt and thread for my mother. The store was more than four kilometers away, and had to follow narrow paths since there were no roads to speak of.

During this period of growing up, my mother's health kept declining. By the time I was four years old, I was witnessing my mother spitting blood in a glass jar. Medical care was very poor- difficult to attain, inefficient, and primitive. What few doctors existed, they were poorly educated and trained, and most of the time indifferent. They were given a commission after graduation and working for the government. The doctor that examined my mother a few times kept insisting that she had malaria and kept prescribing quinine, although he sent her for an x-ray in the city of Cosenza- some forty kilometers away. While going for x-rays (i ragi) she was to bring the blood mixed sputum in the glass jar.

For mama to get to the train for Cosenza, she had to walk down a steep hill, some 200-300 meters, to the road below, then start walking 4 kilometers to the station. If she was lucky, the mail bus would be running and she would get a ride, otherwise continued walking. When she got to Cosenza, she walked to the hospital, approximately one kilometer. Then returning that afternoon, late usually, she had to repeat the same route sick as she was. At the hospital in Cosenza they suspected she might be coming down with tuberculosis, and for her to tell her doctor. She did and the doctor still treated her for malaria for the next four years.

Meanwhile in the United States my father had started his own business as an independent landscape gardener, learned to drive, and became a US citizen in early 1929, when I was five years old.

In December 1929, before Christmas, he returned to Italy to check on his wife and children, and to see if he could make arrangements to bring his family to the US. He was not successful due to much red tape. That was the first time I had seen my father, since I was born seven months after he embarked for America in 1923. On this trip while he was home in Italy he purchased a larger piece of land approximately 32 acres (8 hectares) in the district of Mangino, approximately 1 and one-half kilometers from the present residence. The house was much larger, two rooms and a kitchen, and the land wasn't as steep.

My father returned to America early February 1930, to get back to work and we moved in the new location in June that same year. At this location now we could have more animals- goats, pigs, and chickens. As soon as we moved we built a chicken coop, two pig pens and a barn. My sister, eight years old, and myself, a little over six years old were given the chores of taking care of the animals, with my mother's help.

Schooling and education was another chore that we had to deal with, and my mother, although illiterate, made sure that we went to school. My sister, being two years older, started school in 1928, at six years of age. The rural school was one room, with four grades being taught simultaneously by one teacher. To get to school, we walked one and one-half kilometers, three narrow paths, three wooded areas and a steep, 300 meter hill to get to a gravel road. Then walk another one-half kilometer to the school. For safety purposes children within one kilometer would meet at a particular point and then walk to school together.

I was introduced to school in 1929, when I was five years old. My mother made my sister take me with her to school. I was put on a bench in the back of the room with a pencil and piece of lined, thin sheet of yellow paper, and was shown how to draw straight vertical lines all day long. I thought I was a genius! The next day we had to bring a nickel to pay for the pencil.

The following year, 1930, we moved to the new farm that my father had bought the previous year, and a new school. This school was only one-half kilometer away. It was a one room mud brick house, with two open holes for windows; no sash or glass, but two homemade shutters for bad weather. The two square, open windows were the only source of light. The only source of sanitation was a mud brick outhouse, with no water or washing facilities. Again four grades in one room and one teacher. The subjects were taught on three and two hour periods. One subject was from 8 AM to 11 AM, the second subject from 1 PM to 3 PM. We got up at 5 AM, did chores in the farm before, in between classes and after school each day. Boys, starting at the age of eight, were required to do military training, once per week for farm boys and three times a week plus half a day on Saturdays for boys living in a town or city. These boys were called Balilla (junior fascists). These times were Benito Mussolini's times. All students had to pay a 5 lira tax (or tessara) each year, at beginning of school years. Every household or farm equipment and tools were taxed, including a pen knife, ax, and/or a hoe.

Living under a dictatorship, there was no access to world news, or popular magazines or books to read. The only thing available was what Mussolini decided to print, or allowable to be said or broadcast. There were no radios or telephones in rural areas. In the town of St. Marco there may have been half a dozen radios, which only the elite and loyal government supporters were allowed to have, and one telephone located in the municipal building.

In 1933, Mussolini confiscated every family's gold wedding bands, to support his military buildup in anticipation of conquering Ethiopia. In return he gave in exchange a horse shoe nail shaped into a ring. That was supposed to show patriotism.

Life was not easy. Although my mother was sick, most of the time she never stopped working hard, going to town on foot on Sunday, taking my sister and I with her. Sunday was Church day, but also market day, where farmers and trader people bring their products and wares to sell, trade or buy. Many times when my mother had to deal with other farmers, or had things to take care of in town, she would leave us with either neighbors, babysitters, or relatives for the day. And yes, according to today's standards, I had my share of child abuse, not from my family but from others that were supposed to take care of me.

So was life until my mother passed away when I was ten years old. During the time mother was alive, she worked hard every day of her life, and we followed in step. My sister and I helped raising livestock, plant vegetables and fruit trees, pick olives and figs and acorns, and clean the chicken coops, pig pens, and barn. At eight years old I was helping my paternal uncle with the sowing of wheat by driving teams of oxen and horses while he was holding the plow.

This was done while raining and I was ankle deep in mud. I was also harnessing donkeys and a horse, and herding livestock; and we managed to get some schooling! Not much to brag about. The only time we did homework was at night by the light of a homemade oil lamp, and the light of an open fire. My mother being illiterate could not in any way help us. My father in the United States never forgot us for a moment. A letter would always come at least twice a month, and whenever he could he would send Mama a little money.

In December 1932 my father came back to Italy once again with the intentions and hope of bringing his family to America. He would always come in the winter because there was no work for him in his trade during the cold winter. He tried getting papers through both the Italian and American Consulates but got nowhere because of my mother's condition. Mother's tuberculosis was quite advanced, and some days she could not do any work regardless of how hard she would try. The medical care she was receiving was totally inadequate and backwards. There were no medical care facilities where we lived and the doctors were inadequate and totally deficient. My father returned back to the US in early February 1933, with the promise he would return and try again until he succeeded.

In 1934 my father applied for passports through the Italian Consulate in New York City for his family to come to America. In the meantime my mother became seriously ill by fall of 1934 and by October she was bedridden. My father returned to Italy the 3rd of December 1934, and he had his last Christmas with his beloved wife and children. My mother passed away on January 18th, 1935; I was 10 years old, my sister 12 years old. Again, the passports were not forthcoming.

After my mother's passing my father decided that he was not going to leave us alone in the farm, but going to place us where we could get a little better education.

He arranged for me to go to the St. Marco schools, and live in a boarding house run by a supposedly former school professor and his wife. My sister, he was able to place her in a convent school run by a religious order in Cosenza, some 40 kilometers away. He did all this before he returned to the United States in mid February 1935. One of my uncles, the husband of my Father's sister, would take care of the farm. The expense would be paid by proceeds from the farm.

Before I go any further, I would like to mention that at seven years of age I had my own ax and hoe so that I could be responsible for gathering and chopping wood for the house. The hoe, so that my sister and I could take care of the vegetable garden, and do general weeding and other chores.

I believe my mother knew that she did not have long to live, and wanted to make sure that we were prepared to take care of ourselves. By eight years old my sister and I could handle most of the house chores. I could handle livestock, cleaning stables, pig pens, chicken coops, and small house repairs. I was not alone in these areas. Most of the farm children in the nearby farms had to do the same. I could harness a donkey by age eight and a horse by age nine- with the help of a tree stump in the front of the barn. I could ride both bareback or harnessed, both a donkey and a horse. Our days were full, from five AM to nine PM everyday; We still managed to get some schooling.

Going back to my living in a boarding house in St. Marco. The house was attached to other buildings, as usually are in most of the cities and towns in Italy and most, if not all, of Europe. It was owned by people who considered themselves above the masses, especially farmers (Contadini). Although, they would all have starved to death if it hadn't been for the farmers. They considered themselves elites or high class, maybe because they hardly ever worked, especially manual work. There was definitely class distinction, and plenty of bias.

My two years' stay was not pleasant but in some ways fruitful.

The town boys, and many adults were quite abusive with name-calling and epithets to me for being a farm boy. I was not streetwise like the town kids; therefore to them I was a misfit. My greatest desire after I began school in town was to learn, after I was exposed to school books and a real school room with a single class in it. My learning in the farm was minimal, so when I started in town I was placed in the 2nd grade. I was afraid that I was too old to be in this grade, but soon found out there were older children than me in the class. As a matter of fact, there was one boy fourteen years old who was repeating the second grade for the third time. He was a boy from inside the town.

My new professor (teacher) was an elderly man, with thick eye glasses by the name of Aieta, and a very serious and dedicated teacher. He received me very politely, asked me where I came from and where I had gone to school. I told him everything, including that I had lost my mother, and my father was in another country. He thanked me, informed me of the school rules, and what he expected from his pupils, and that he would always be available if I needed help. He probably anticipated that the town children would make fun of me, so he seated me in front of the classroom. When he handed me two school books for me to learn from, I was absolutely elated and delighted. During these times all books were government owned, and were issued for the duration of the grade period, then returned. One of the two books was Italian two and three, the other was Italian history. A day later I would get another one, mathematics. Aside from about half a dozen children who wanted to learn, the other nineteen or twenty had no such inclination, and were forever being punished for being disorderly and disruptive. The punishment usually consisted of being hit several times in the palm of the hand with a ruler or a switch.

Not only children of the town called me all kinds of names, but so some of the town's so-called elites. One of the names I was referred to was "tamarro," which meant ignorant peasant, or a hick. A lot of these children were so-called "upper class," and some of them were streetwise, street-roaming urchins.

After about one week professor Aieta began to sort of cater to me and he got to like me because I really wanted to learn, and he realized that. By the way he was Jewish, very learned, and some kids in school would make remarks such as the "blind Abrei," the Jewish blind. I liked him also, because he really was a great teacher.

Before the end of the spring semester in 1935, he was introducing me to third and fourth grade material. I was very lucky that the following semester he was promoted to teach the third grade and I was in his class once again. I only did the first semester of second grade, and moved to the second semester of the third grade in the following semester, fall semester. He would take me aside after class and teach me decimals and fractions. He trusted me so much that he'd have me take care of his personal transactions at the post office and bank during lunch and off hours. One day during the fall semester he took me aside, and told me that he would show me how the universe worked. I had no idea what he had in mind. He told me to stay after school, and I did. When all the other students had left, he took me into a locked room, full or I should say with everything covered with dust. You could not see through the dirty glass of the windows. Anyway he took me to a table with a large object covered with a dusty cloth. In removing that cover, he revealed a working model of the universe- every piece, including the gears were made of copper. Having not been used and taken care of, everything was oxidized but still working. When turning a crank, it showed the sun and all the planets revolving. It was the most beautiful thing I had seen, the first time that I was exposed to science. That experience has been the first and most lasting in my life, even though at the time I had very little or no understanding of what it was all about.

During the summers I went back to the farm. I spent half the summer with my uncle working on our farm, and the other half with my maternal grandparents working in their farm. In 1936 I started my fourth grade in town, back at the boarding house. I had a new professor, next door to Professor Aieta, who never forgot me, and I never forgot him. Many times during lunch and after hours he'd teach me math and beginning of physics. The math I mostly understood but physics was a start for the future. It did open my mind to new ideas and thoughts.

As far as my boarding went, it was not a pleasant experience. The owner, so-called professor, came from a formerly prominent family, but because of excesses and irresponsible life styles, they became destitute. He called himself a professor, but actually I don't believe he went beyond the equivalent of high school in the country. But during the early 1900's that was sufficient to teach in elementary schools. As I understand he was not a worker, and didn't last long as a teacher. Although he got married and had a family, he lived by sponging off his family. When his family ended he resorted to boarding. The house where he lived, and used as a boarding home, was actually owned by his wife's family.

The house had no heating or cooling facilities, just a couple of windows on each floor, with no screening for summer cooling. Flies and other creatures were everywhere. There were three other boarders besides myself and we lived and slept in the same room downstairs. We had one large table on one side with a single light bulb hanging over it, for all of us to do our homework, and general use. Two of the boys were from another town without a formal school, and were "elite" families. The third boarder was my paternal cousin, whose father, my uncle, was well-to-do. Therefore my cousin had never done any manual work. And there I was, the "tamarro" among them. The "professor" made sure to remind me that I was the peasant, "tamarro," on a daily basis. Food was very minimal and simple. I was more or less like a servant when I wasn't in school. I was asked to do whatever chores were around. Several times I ran away, usually to the convent of St. Anthony, which was less than half a kilometer away. A few times I ran away to my maternal grandparents, some ten kilometers away. Each time, if at the convent, the Father would calm me down and walk me back to the boarding house. When at my grandparents, my uncle, my mother's youngest brother, would take me back to the boarding house. They brought me back not because of respect to the owner of the boarding house, but because they didn't want me to miss school.

The Father at the convent was an ordained monk, extremely well-educated, kind man. His name was Father Ubaldo, order of St. Anthony, and was a great help to me both spiritually and scholastically. He was always willing and eager to help, and yes, I went hungry while I stayed at that boarding house.

My maternal grandfather, Nonno Giuseppe (Grandfather Joseph), was a tough little man- no taller than five feet- but very kind and loving. He was in his eighties, he liked wine and usually noticed everything around him. When I came to his farm in the summer of 1935, after five months at the boarding home, he noticed that I had lost weight and asked me why. I sort of lied a little and told him because of the three nights a week of military training, one night a week Catechism training and school in general. I don't think he bought it. Anyway while I was with my grandparents, I worked in the farm and at the same time they tried to fatten me up. About two weeks after I had returned to the town, one Sunday around 11 o'clock in the morning my grandfather arrived at the boarding house with a small linen bag filled with eggs packed in straw. He had walked over ten kilometers alone to bring eggs to his grandson. The owners of the boarding house took the eggs without even offering this tired old man a glass of water. He turned around and started back. I went with him and asked if he had eaten. He said yes, he had brought food with him and had water to drink at the public fountain at the entrance of the town. I turned around at the professor, and told him I was going back with my grandfather and we left for the ten kilometer trek back. It took us six hours of walking to the farm. That's what you would call class bias or discrimination. Next morning my maternal uncle Ralph took me back to St. Marco on horseback. I never saw a trace of the eggs that my grandfather had brought for me, and so I told my grandparents and uncle.

At this point I should like to tell you about my maternal grandparents. My grandfather, Giuseppe Lecce, was born around 1847-1850; and my grandmother, Maddalene Argondezza was born around 1850-1857. Both were of Albanian origin- three or four generations back. Their ancestors formed their own Albanian communities when they arrived from Albania, and followed ancestral customs and language. Those communities, now called Paese or Towns, still exist and many of their customs are still followed and practiced. However, they all also speak the Italian language.

My grandmother was married possibly in late 1870's to someone from the same town, and left Italy soon after for South America, Brazil I believe, to work in land development or mines as a laborer. My grandfather, as a young man also left for South America in the mid seventies to better himself. He was a shepherd all his life and also did farm work. So he went to Argentina to make money as a farm hand and also to work in the mines.

Within less than two years in Brazil, grandmother's husband became ill and died, leaving my illiterate grandmother with a small child alone. We must remember that both Grandmother and Grandfather were uneducated and illiterate, as were 85 to 90 % of all the immigrants going overseas. So my grandmother and baby daughter headed back for home, Mongrassano, Italy, where they originally came from. My grandfather, meanwhile, having made a little money and being tired of the hard work and being abused like slaves by the bosses, headed home to Mongrasano also, at about the same time. They ended up on the same dirty ship going home, steerage of course. During these days if you traveled steerage, they gave each passenger daily rations and everyone had to cook for themselves, in a common kitchen.

My grandfather, although a rough and probably unmannered man, felt sorry for the woman alone with a baby and helped her all the way home. He was single and alone, she was a widow with a baby girl, and talking it over, they decided to get married, and look for a homestead. During this period the government encouraged people to acquire an undeveloped piece of land as a homestead. That's how my maternal grandparents became farmers in the district of Stamile, some ten kilometers south of the town of St. Marco, and some eighteen kilometers from their hometown of Mongrassano. As far as I can figure, they became homesteaders in the early or mid 1880's. Between 1888 and 1896 they had four children, three boys- Pietro, Domenico, Raffaele, and Rosa in 1896, my mother.

Now going back to my life in St. Marco. After summer vacation at my grandparents' farm, I returned to the boarding house and school in town. The first week in September I reported to my third grade class. The professor was strict but fair, and managed the class like a professional, but I felt sorry for him. Half the boys in the class were disruptive, and with the punishment doled out to them, the teacher still ended up throwing them out of the class. It seemed that it followed the same pattern each day for about a week. Finally he reported them to the fascist cadre that ran the military training three times per week, and Saturday morning, for disciplinary action. We must remember that this period was dominated by Benito Mussolini, and every child, especially boys, had to attend school and military training. When I went to school, and walked in town, I still had to take the abuse by the ignorant, both common and elite, hecklers. Although it annoyed and bothered me, I just learned to ignore them. After a few months they finally gave up, at least most of them. I worked as hard as I could and the teachers, both Aieta and the present one, gave me all the help I asked for. I did so well that my third grade began in September and ended in December 1935. In January 1936 I started my fourth grade. Life in town was the same, more or less. I did well in school, bad in the boarding house, and I ran away several times to my grandparents for a good meal. I walked the ten kilometers each time, once in the dark. The only difference this year was that my paternal aunt Emilia and her husband and son Gaetano took me to the seashore for a two week vacation. I had never seen the sea, and it really was an experience walking in the sand and going in the salt water.

In September 1936, I returned back to town to finish fourth grade. I had to ask my uncle to buy another Balilla uniform (Junior Fascists) because the director of military training (a Fascist officer, of course) didn't like the way my present suit fitted. That was done in quick order.

In October 1936, we received a letter from my father in the US that he had been at the Italian embassy in New York City and had applied for passports to the USA for me and my sister. Also he informed us that he would return to Italy before Christmas, and would try to bring me and my sister to America in February, if everything went well with the passports. Because we lived in Italy and we were only Italian citizens, we could travel only on Italian passports. Although the American Embassy in Italy helped in expediting the issue of the passports, since my father was an American citizen.

I left school and the boarding house in November and stayed with my grandparents and maternal uncle. My father returned to Italy the first week of December 1936, with plans to bring my sister and I to the United States this time.

As soon as he arrived in St. Marco Argentano, my father went directly to the municipal building (government building) and contacted the Italian and American embassies about the passports. They acknowledged that the applications were on file, but hadn't acted on them yet. My father insisted on the urgency of getting them as soon as possible, if possible before February 1937. In the meantime, just before Christmas, he had to make a few trips by train to Naples' Italian embassies office and bribe a few people there, so that the passports would be issued in time.

Our stay with Mama's parents was happy and sad. We were happy that we were all together, and very sad at the thought that we would be separated, probably not to see each other again.

The day that my father came back, I was at my grandparents' home helping my grandfather repair a pig pen, which was built of mud bricks and had been damaged by wind and rain. As he arrived, that late afternoon, at my grandparents' home, he found me knee deep in mud and straw, mixing it to repair the pig pen. He came directly at me and gave me a big hug- mud and all.

The reason my father wanted the passports, and to book passage in February or before, was that my birthday was in March, and I would have been 13 years old. Mussolini, Italy's dictator, would not allow any boy 13 years or age or older to leave the country. As it would happen, father got a notice from the municipal building the last week of January 1937, that the passports were ready in the Naples embassy's office, and he could go and pick them up and book passage on the S. S. Rex, one of the newest steamships. After making another trip to Naples and bribing a few hands, the job was done.

When my father returned from Naples, the next important job was to get us some decent traveling clothes. In Italy during those days, clothes had to be made. There were no stores that you could go and buy ready-made clothes. So a few days before the end of January, my father took us to a tailor in town. He took measurements and in less than two weeks we had traveling clothes.

Now came the hardest part, parting and leaving the loved ones behind. We spent most of our time before leaving with my grandparents, who we loved and they loved us more than anything. The rainy season had begun, and everything was drenched, and we spent most if not all our time indoors. In some way this was good because it kept us all together.

My father during this time would come and stay with us during the middle of the day and the rest of the time he would stay at his sister, my aunt's, house- working out business arrangements for taking care of our farm after we were gone.

The day we had to leave, my father came to pick us up at my grandparents' house early in the morning. Both of my grandparents were sad, and grandmother was crying because she would lose us, but she made a wonderful meal. None of us ate too much, but we tried to stay as cheerful as we could. My father was always fond of mama's parents, and they loved my father from the first day they met him.

We had to get to the railroad station by 7:00 pm, so at about 11:00 am, we had to sadly say goodbye to my grandparents and leave by foot in a heavy rain and try to make the 3 ½- 4 kilometer walk to my uncle and aunt's home. To accomplish this, we had to travel through two valleys and over two pretty steep hills, and through paths between people's properties. We had to cross over a stream or gully, which normally would have been around three or four inches of water. The gully was now about two meters wide and approximately two or two and a half meters high. When we approached it, with all the rain coming down, the water level was almost to the top, approximately two meters high. There was no way that we could have crossed it on foot. My father looked around the farms and along the stream and saw a big tree that had been uprooted. He asked me to help, and dragged it across the gully. The branches held it in place and prevented it from turning. My father was wearing rubber boots that he had brought with him from America. He picked up my sister in his arms, and, with me crying, he carried her on the other side. He came back and did the same with me. God was with us, because one slip and that would have been the end. That was my father! A little shaky, the three of us walked the additional kilometer to my uncle and aunt's house.

Everything was packed and ready to go. The only baggage we had was a traveler's trunk that my father had brought with him from the USA. One special item was packed into that trunk, a bolt of linen cloth; it was made from flax grown by us, picked by us, processed by us, and woven into cloth on an old hand-operated loom by my mother and her mother. We still have most of it in a bolt as it was originally folded. The trunk was loaded in the rear of the horse buggy; my uncle hitched the horse to the buggy, we said goodbye to my aunt and cousin, got into the buggy, me sitting on my father's lap, and left for the railroad station.

We got to the station at about 6:30 PM, one and a half hours before train time. All the time during the day it was pouring rain, as it was when we got to the station. My uncle proposed that while waiting, we go to the small café-restaurant located right next to the railroad station and have a farewell drink and something to eat, on him. We did and he ordered mortatella salami, beer for the adults and wine for me and my sister. It was a nice goodbye! At 8:00 we boarded the train after another round of sad goodbyes, and shedding a few more tears.

From the St. Marco-Roggiano Station we traveled approximately fifty kilometers to Castrovillare, a central railroad switching depot. Within one hour we switched to the Naples line, with another car switch at Battipaglia, a major railroad depot and switching center, located near Salerno. The last leg was to Naples. The trip took us fifteen hours, in the most uncomfortable, all-wood interior rail car. The seats were all wood, and the inside damp, almost wet and cold. All the way it poured heavy rain. For a bathroom, there was an enclosure at one corner of the car, with a hole in the floor, in which you could watch the rails go by. This of course was third class travel, the best we could afford. The trip took fifteen hours. Today, the same trip takes six hours.

We arrived in Naples after 11:00 in the morning. My father bargained with a horse-drawn taxi to drive us to a reasonably priced hotel, close to the piers. As soon as we got to the hotel, my father took us to eat in a trattoria (diner-restaurant sort of), near the hotel. Then we went to the Italian Embassy which was not too far from the piers, and we got the once over by a uniformed officer (fascist of course), and kept talking to my father while constantly looking at me. Finally they told him that we could leave, but return in the morning. By this time it was after 4:00 in the afternoon of February 17th. We were dead tired but father tried to be cheerful and jovial, but young as I was, I sensed he was worried. We went back to the hotel, washed up and rested for awhile, after which we went back to that same trattoria to eat. We had never before eaten in a restaurant, and my father kept telling me and my sister Giulia how to act in the restaurant in front of other people. It was a learning experience of a lifetime.

Next morning, February 18th, 1937, we ate at that same place, and my father took us to the American Embassy before going again to the Italian Embassy. He explained what had expired the previous day, and asked them if they could help out in expediting the approval of his children's passports. Without the Italian Embassy's official stamp on the passports, we would not be able to board the ship to America the next day. The official spoke to my father and promised to help, since my father was an American citizen. We left the American Embassy and went directly to the Italian Embassy. Again we were met by that fascist official, but this time he went inside a big office with two officials, who asked my father several questions, then came over to me and asked me my name, was that man my father, who was the girl with us, then asked me if I had Balilla training and did I really want to go to America. I looked at my father and he told me to answer all the questions truthfully. I did. Then the man behind the desk asked my father for our passports and he stamped the passports right over our pictures, with an embossing stamp. This was accomplished just before the Embassy closed for their afternoon siesta. We got back to the hotel after 1:00 PM, went to eat at the same place, and rested the rest of the afternoon. I still have that passport.

The next day, February 19th, was the day that we would board the S.S. Rex for America. Ships would leave for the USA every two weeks from Naples to New York City. The ships making this trip were the S. S. Rex, S. S. Conte di Savoia, S. S. Vulcania, and S. S. Saturnia. The Rex and Conti di Savoia, were the newest and fastest of the fleet.

February 19th, we got up early, went to eat and left for the pier where the S. S. Rex was docked. We got there at 9:00, went into a huge waiting room with dozens of people of all means. The common or poor people on the one side with wooden benches, the first and second class people on the other side with chairs and tables. We traveled third class so we were on the common side. When we got there, they were already checking and boarding first class, next came second class and at about 10:30 – 11:00 they started processing the third class passengers, the largest group. Our turn came at about 11:30. We were led up the gangplank into the ship and were told to stop by some of Mussolini's blackshirts, on the deck by the gang-plank. The official told my father to go with him off the ship, and left me and my sister on the ship by the gangplank. My father asked one of the sailors to please look after us, and that he would return in a few minutes. Of course we were scared stiff and started crying. Near 12 noon they started untying the ropes of the gangplank and father was nowhere to be seen. I told my sister to stay and I ran off the ship to look for father. As I got off I saw my father running up the stairs of the gang plank. He grabbed my hand and we ran towards the ship. When we got there the gangplank had been removed approximately one and a half feet. My father grabbed my hand real tight and told me to jump onto the ship. We did, and as we did two sailors grabbed our arms and pulled us safely into the ship, with my sister crying her little heart out. That was my escape from Mussolini.

The reason they got my father off the ship was to confiscate what little money he had. He had on him $250, and they confiscated $200 off him. He had to beg them to leave some money to take care of us. Since they could not prevent me from leaving Italy, they punished my father by taking his money.

Finally we were on our way to America. We were a little scared being on this huge boat and at sea. After all, we were farm folks, and me and my sister being landlubber farmers this was a bit scary. However, after we got to our cabin, nice and clean and with bathrooms right next door, we felt a little better. The cabin consisted of one bed and two bunk beds, and a small table, and drawers in the wall. The weather as usual was nasty- rain and wind- as we got under way. After about one hour my father wanted us to go on deck and see what the sea looked like and also to get some fresh air. By the time we went up deck, the land was far away, and the Mediterranean was really rough, with five to seven foot waves. Needless to say, before we reached Gibraltar my sister and I were miserably sea sick, and so were a lot of the other passengers. Very few went to dinner that evening. The ship, even third class, was beautiful, everything polished and clean,. The ship had a very nice dining room, statues and beautiful pictures on the walls. Half of the first night was terrible, being sea sick and all, but we slept well the second half. Next morning we had a nice breakfast, and started to feel better. I think the seasickness was partly from fear and partly from the rough seas. In less than two and a half days we passed the Azore Islands, and we went up on the deck and watched as we went by. Some fishermen in dories waved at us and we waved back. Still within sight of the Islands, we saw for the first time huge fish partially above water. My father thought they were rige (whales) or boa (dolphins). From here on we had a very nice trip. I learned how to go up the various stairs of the ship looking for other children to play with, went on deck watching the sea go by- it was a new world for me. A couple of nights we listened to an orchestra playing classical and popular music, and some man singing American songs. My sister and I knew absolutely no English words, but we listened with great interest anyway.

The only event of interest that happened during the trip was that I mistakenly patronized the ladies' restroom instead of the mens'. It seemed that when the ship came to America from Italy, all the signs aboard were in English, and when it returned from America to Italy all the signs were in Italian. Now the Italian word for men is *uomo* and for women's *gentile donna*. So when I saw the word "Gentleman" I assumed it was ladies. The whole trip I never got caught, except by my father the last day of the voyage. Needless to say, I got my first lesson on the English language. The other event was that on the 25th of February 1937, while still at sea, me and my sister became US citizens, through derivation of my father's citizenship. Two days before we disembarked at N.Y. City. The advantage of this was that we did not have to go through immigration screening. On the 27th of February we disembarked like American citizens.

We got off the ship at 11:30 in the morning, in a light rain mixed with snow. The pier was wet and dirty, with dozens of black men unloading the baggage. For us it was a new experience because we had never seen black men before. Most of them were chewing gum, and we asked my father why they were chewing like cows and goats. My poor father had a lot to explain to us about the new world. Since we had eaten breakfast at six o'clock in the morning, my father treated us to a new food for lunch- hot dogs from a vendor on the pier, with sauerkrauts and all. We liked them and it was our first treat in America.

While waiting for the luggage, my father started asking the taxicab drivers if they would take us to Baldwin, LI for $25, that was the most he could afford, since his total wealth at this time was $35. After several inquiries, a young taxi driver said he would take us. He tied the trunk on the rack in back of the taxi, we got in and he drove us to Baldwin to a house which my father had made arrangements to rent. It really was an apartment in a private house; one large room, a large kitchen and an unheated porch. We separated the big room with a large blanket, one half being my sister's bed quarters and the other half me and my father's. The landlord was a retired navy seaman, and was a very kind and nice man. The next door neighbors were a family, countrymen from the same town in Italy, that knew my father quite well. They were very helpful in doing the shopping and helping us set up the living arrangements.

As soon as we arrived in Baldwin, my father went to the bank, to borrow some money for us to buy bedding, towels, kitchen utensils, and some groceries. Luckily one of the bank officials was a customer of my father and vouched for my father in getting a loan. My father was well-known and well-liked by many people in the community. Next door neighbors helped with the shopping. The brother of the neighbor had a half ton pickup truck, and by seven o'clock that evening we were all settled in. We did all our shopping at discount stores in the next town, Freeport, which was about one mile away.

The next day, Saturday, my father started briefing me about his work. First, he had bought a half ton Ford Model A truck, which had been lying idle for the last three months, in the cold, rain, and snow. So he was going to show me how to start it. We cleaned the windshield, managed to open the doors, and he tried to start, but the battery couldn't start. He told me to get behind the steering wheel and hold the magneto lever at a certain position, showed me the choke lever and told me how to move it when the engine got started. He went in the front of the car with a good-sized crank, started cranking the motor until it started, and I kept jiggling the choke lever the way he had shown, and the engine kept going. I had never been in back of a car's steering wheel in my life, and I was sort of scared. Once the motor kept running my father got in the back of the steering wheel and we went for a short ride to the gas station to have the battery charged. My first work adventure in America.

The gas station was actually just across the street, a Gulf gasoline station. I was fascinated watching the owner-mechanic check the antifreeze, the water in the radiator, and putting air in the tires with the free-air stand in the corner of the garage. This was my first time that I was made aware of compressed air. The next most fascinating operation was watching the mechanic drive cars over an open pit to change the oil and lubricating, even though it was snowing. Needles to say, I would be making many trips to that gas station to watch the mechanic work.

The next thing my father did was to go to all his customers to let them know that he was back. Since we had no telephone, he did it in person. During these days there were few houses with telephones. In a few days he started getting messages in the mail asking him to do cleaning jobs, and the pruning and cutting. In the weekends he would take me with him to help, and also to meet his customers. This gave my father the chance to make some money. Also many times after school, he would pick me up and I would work with him until it got dark. Almost all his customers were wonderful to me and my sister, and definitely very helpful.

Saint Marco Argentano, Calabria Italy

1916-1920: Father Angelo—Italian
Army WWI

1924: Father Angelo in the USA.

1925 : Family - Paternal grandmother
Giusephina with sister Giulia,
Mother Rosa, and me Dario at 16
monts old.

1928 : Mother Rosa, me 4 years
old, and My sister Giula
6 years old.

1929 - My father Angelo. gardener in
Baldwin L.I., N.Y

1929 - Mother Rosa

1929 - Mama Rosa, me 5 years old,
Sister Giulia 7 years old.

December 1929 - Mama Rosa
And Father Angelo in front of
Hospital, Cosenza, Italy.

1929 - Aunt Emilia, mother Rosa,
Me, Giulia and cousin Gaetano

1931 - From left to right: sister Giulia,
Me 7, maternal grandmother,
Maddalena, And Mother Rosa.

1931 - Sister Giulia's first communion.

1932 - Madonna of the Pettiruto, Saint Sosti, Italy.

December 1932 - me Dario, in Napoli, Italy- Father took me with him trying to apply for Passports to America.

Mama's tomb, S.Marco Argentano, Italy.

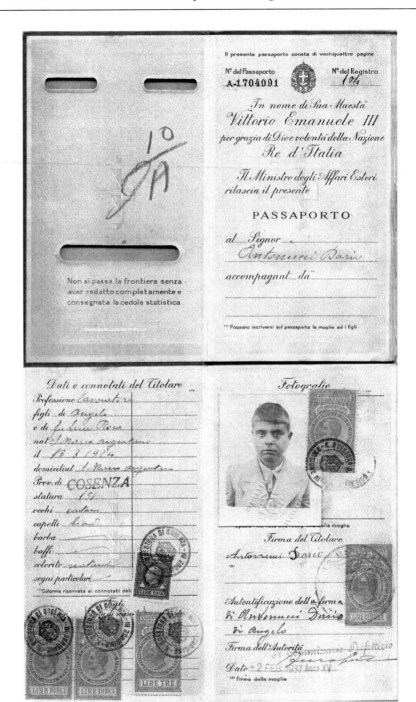

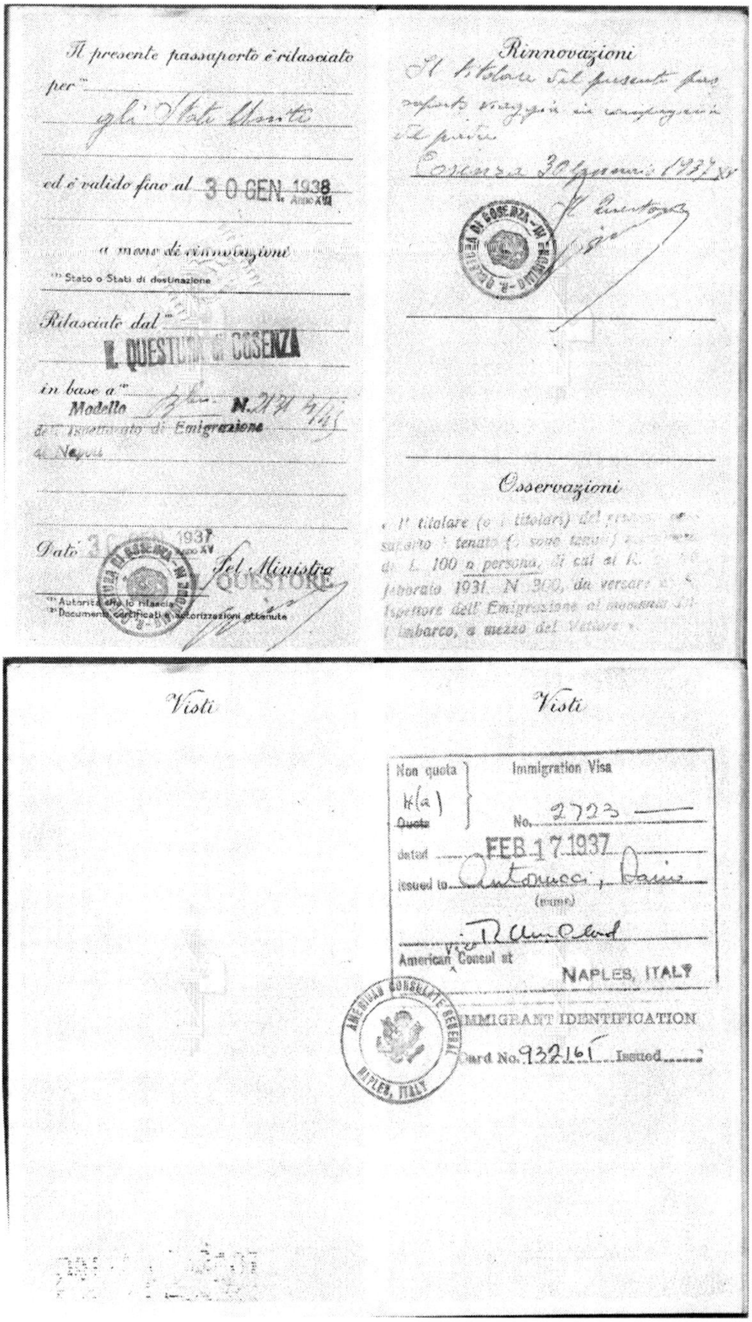
Il presente passaporto è rilasciato per
gli Stati Uniti
ed è valido fino al 30 GEN. 1938
a meno di rinnovazioni
Stato o Stati di destinazione
Rilasciato dal
R. QUESTURA DI COSENZA
in base a
Modello N.
dell' Ispettorato di Emigrazione di Napoli
Dato 30 GEN. 1937 Anno XV
Pel Ministro
IL QUESTORE
Autorità che lo rilascia
Documenti, certificati e autorizzazioni ottenute
Rinnovazioni
Cosenza 30 gennaio 1937
Osservazioni
Visti
Visti
Non quota
Quota
Immigration Visa
No. 2723
dated FEB 17 1937
issued to
(name)
American Consul at NAPLES, ITALY
AMERICAN CONSULATE GENERAL NAPLES, ITALY
IMMIGRANT IDENTIFICATION
Card No. 932161 Issued

My first impression of America

I was totally overwhelmed, after we landed, at the crowds of people and the tall buildings in New York, the indifference of people to each other in the streets, and the overabundance of automobiles and trucks. I was also surprised and overwhelmed at the snow. Where we came from in southern Italy, we very seldom saw snow, except far away on the top of mountains.

When we reached Baldwin, Long Island, we were surprised at all the wooden houses, the concrete and paved streets, the sidewalks, and at the many stores, and most of all at the central heating and gas cooking stove. In Italy, the houses in town were all bricks or concrete, and in the country of mud bricks. Another thing we were surprised by was the flatness of the land.

Our reaction in meeting American people was somewhat enlightening. Most of the people we met at first were very nice. Some of them, a few, must have thought were kind of freaks because of the language, and shyness. They didn't quite understand why we didn't speak or understand English. Most, if not all, of my father's customers, both men and women, wanted to see us and meet with us as soon as possible. Some wanted us to go to their houses to meet. Many offered us items for the house and/or clothing to wear. They were really wonderful and all of them that we met tried to teach us words by demonstration. One couple, an elderly Jewish couple, went as far as getting me and my sister a subscription to the National Geographic magazine. Today, 71 years later, we still receive this magazine.

Learning the American way:

Since we were small children, my mother would always tell us, "Learn all and everything you can and always look up to people who are better than you, and always remember that your name and reputation are your most valued possessions." After my mother died, my father took over and reminded us all the time of the same things. We tried to live by these values. So after we came to America we tried to always remember and live by these values. When we met people we always tried to smile and be polite, even when some of them tried to make fun of us at the beginning. We tried to follow the way American people lived and acted, even though at times it was not exactly the right way. After we began schooling and began to learn the language we began to discriminate somewhat.

My father, as soon as the weather improved, taught me about lawnmowers, cutting grass, edge and bush trimming, transplanting, and learning the art of shopping and getting familiar with different stores and products. My sister did the washing and cooking, and we both worked in keeping the house clean and orderly. I kept the small yard well-trimmed and clean.

As soon as we got to Baldwin, the subject of education became of main interest. We arrived to the United States on Friday, February 27th and my father brought us to school on Monday, March 2nd, 1937. My sister and I held hands, and felt very scared. The principal of elementary school No. 3, a Mr. Ducker, greeted us in his office and my father registered us. They placed us in the fourth grade with a Mrs. Trudy McDermot, one of two fourth grade teachers who knew my father well. She and her husband were customers of my father. None of the staff in the school, nor any of the children, spoke or understood Italian, and we didn't know a single word of English, except for "ladies" and "gentlemen." Bilingual teaching was unheard of during these days!

We were left in a very awkward predicament, as was the teacher. We sat down on the side of the class while the teacher thought of something for us to do. In the meanwhile she started the class, by all the students rising, as we followed, and pledged allegiance to the flag. Since we had to do the same in Italian school, it was the first lesson we learned and understood. After the class started the teacher gave assignments to the students to do, but picked a boy and girl, told them to get their coats, as she signaled us to do the same, and take me and my sister in the school yard and teach us words by demonstration. Dorothy took me by the hand, Ronald took my sister by the hand, and we went outside. It was a nice sunny and cold day. Each of the students picked up a stone from the ground, and showing it to us said, "say stone." We answered back and said "no e uno" (no it's one). The problem being that the word "say" in English is the same pronunciation as "sei" (six) in Italian. Anyway, Dorothy and Ronald finally decided to pick up an object or item from the ground and told us what it was without saying "say." It was a long school day, but we learned the names of stone, orange, grass, tree, and paper.

When we got home that afternoon, my father picked us up in his truck, and we told my father of what had happened and he explained that the word "say" meant to repeat. The rest of the week went quite smoothly, considering the situation, and we learned several words. The following week they had kindergarten and first grade picture books for us, and again two fourth grade students were our teachers. By the third week we were being taught how to read and write words with the help of pictures. At the end of the second week my father asked me if I could go to the store, about four blocks from where we lived, and buy him cigarettes and a can of salt. I took the challenge and with a little effort I did it successfully. My father was very proud of me, and I detected tears in his eyes. Yes we were learning the language, and now he didn't have to worry about us.

This procedure of learning continued for about four weeks. As soon as the teacher saw that we were getting along in class pretty well, she started teaching us math and history, also making us copy writing from books and periodicals. My father was able to get a used Italian-English dictionary, and that was a great help. Another excellent source of learning English was the comics section of the newspaper. Dick Tracy, Terry and the Pirates, Smiling Jack and a few others were of great help. By the end of April, academically, we were almost doing as well as the rest of the class. In math I was doing much better than the rest of the class. We already had learned the Pledge of Allegiance and saluting the flag each morning. Being social was another thing.

In Italy, after my mother died, I went to town, and because I was a peasant I was bullied and insulted by the town bullies. In America, because I was a foreigner, especially an Italian, I was bullied, called names, and insulted by the school bullies, especially those in the sixth and seventh grade, and usually of Italian descent. Every time they bullied or insulted me, I became more determined to do better than they. A few times I fought back, especially one time, that resulted in somewhat positive results.

There were three brothers of Italian descent, and three or four followers, that continually antagonized and insulted me and my sister when we came to school in the morning, and in the playground. I kept telling my teacher and the principal several times, and they always promised that they would talk to them and to stop harassing us. This resulted to no effect.

One rainy day walking home from school I stopped at the gas station, which was on the way home, and asked the owner, a very nice man, if I could have a torn inner tire tube. He told me to look in the trash barrel and take whatever I wanted. That I did.

That weekend I went to the woods in back of the house and I found a wild cherry bush with a branch in the shape of a V. I cut it, cleaned it, even removed the bark. Then I found an old discarded shoe and I cut the tongue out of it. I cut two strips out of the tire tube, each about 8-10 inches long, and with the tongue of the shoe and the v fork, I made a sling shot small enough to fit in my back pocked and under my sweater. The next morning on the way to school I partially filled my left pocket with small rocks. I told my sister to go ahead of me to school with her girl friends, and I would follow. As I approached the school, the harassing committee was waiting for me. The leader, named Joe, started to call me "wop" and other not too clean names, as I took my sling shot out and fired a small stone right in his face, as he tried to come to me I loaded my sling shot and aimed it at him. He stopped, turned around crying and followed by his gang, went inside to complain to the principal. The principal ran to me and said not to do that again, and asked for my sling shot. Then he asked me why I did that. I told him why and in broken, very broken, English I told him that I had complained to him and my teacher, and nothing was done to stop the harassment. Anyway he told me to go to my class, and never to do that again. That afternoon he gave me a note to give to my father, and I did. My father told me that I shouldn't have done such a thing, and that the principal, Mr. Ducker, wanted to see him in the morning.

The next morning, he came to school with me to the principal's office, and discussed the situation. My father told the principal that I had told him everything, including the harassment, and that I had told him that I had reported the bullying and bullies to the teacher and principal. The principal said to my father that the school would see that it did not happen again, and gave my father my sling shot for safekeeping. From that day on my sister and I were never bullied or harassed. Years later after I returned from the war I met those three brothers. They were all working for the sanitation department as garbage collectors.

June 1937 came, school ended and I was promoted to the 5th grade for the fall semester. During the summer I worked every day with my father, got books out of the public library, simple books on airplanes, cars, and history and read every night. The comic pages of N.Y. Daily News were studied every day, and especially the Sunday issue.

During the summer my father started to chat about building a house with one of his customers who was a builder. Since my father didn't make too much money, he was looking for an inexpensive house to build. This customer told my father that in the fall he wouldn't be too busy and he probably could build a house for under $4000. My father had a piece of land he had bought at a tax sale in 1933, and even though it used to flood during heavy storms, it still was adequate to build on. By early September, it was decided that the builder would put a five room, one bathroom frame house on that plot for $3800. The house would have asbestos shingle siding, for warmth and durability.

While we lived in the rental house, my father was using the empty lot he owned to propagate trees and bushes. He used cuttings from the trimming of his customers' houses to grow yews, laurels, junipers, Lawson cypress, and a few others. When we moved in our new house in May 1938, my father and I did the landscaping with his own home grown bushes. This work was done after school for me and after a regular working day for my father, and also on weekends and holidays. He did a beautiful job of landscaping, which also served as an example of his trade. Our new home was like a palace to me and my sister, compared with where we came from. Our heating was an automatic fuel oil-fed steam system, and no wood, coal, and ashes to worry about. At a discount furniture store we went shopping and my father bought bedding, a kitchen table with four chairs, and a dining room set with six chairs. The salesman told my father that they were going to have a special Memorial day sale in a week, if he wanted to wait to buy a living room set. We waited, and bought a maple wood frame living room set with a couch and two chairs for around $40, and the salesman threw in an end table for free. This was in the village of Freeport, Long Island- just about 1 ½ miles from Baldwin, our town. Our house was located about three quarters of a mile away from the elementary school, and approximately 1 ½ miles from the junior and high school. This was good, because during these days there were no school busses and it was all walking.

September 1937 came and my sister and I reported to school to begin our 5th grade class. By the way, at home my father insisted speaking to us in his broken English instead of Italian. This worked fine, because when we returned to school we were able to get along with the teachers and students quite well in our broken English. In fifth grade we were able to polish our English, both in writing and speaking the language. By the middle of the semester I could write a story or short essay in almost perfect English, while my spoken English still suffered some. In math I was way ahead of the class. History and civics were coming along quite nicely. The only negative episode came when all of a sudden in the middle of the lesson the fire alarm went off. Not knowing what it was all about, my sister and I were scared so that we turned pale and frightened our teacher. Until now nobody had explained about the fire alarm drill that was periodically run in schools. Anyway, the principal and a teacher took us aside and explained the reason why these drills were done. From then on we took those drills in stride.

After school when my father didn't need me I started doing odd jobs in the neighborhood, sometimes for my father's customers, and got paid for it at twenty-five cents per hour, and many times I got tips also. I did window cleaning, removing and installing windows and door screens, pulling weeds, cleaning leaves off roofs, even cleaning closets, and baby-sitting including changing diapers. When I had made $2.00 my father took me to Baldwin National Bank and made me open a savings account, at age 13. No matter how little I made, my father would make me put it in the savings account. I would walk 1 and ½ miles to the bank to deposit as little as fifty cents at a time. When I had $16.00 in the account, I thought I was the richest guy in town.

At the end of December 1937, when the fifth grade semester ended, I was doing almost as good as the regular students, even better in math, civics, and general science. I was promoted to the sixth grade, instead of staying in the second semester of the fifth grade. During the Christmas recess in 1937, the principal and sixth grade teacher gave me three special books to read: one was English writing and grammar, another was in math (arithmetic), and the third was about the stars and I think Greek mythology. I couldn't read them all during this short period, so I perused through them several times, especially the one about the stars and Greek mythology. Needless to say, when I returned to class in sixth grade in early January, the work was cut out for me, since I intended to keep up with the class no matter what. And I did.

The greatest episode in the sixth grade that enhanced my life very much was when the class went on a field trip to the American Museum of Arts and the planetarium in New York City in the month of April 1938. I was enchanted, flabbergasted, and totally amazed at everything I saw. The planetarium display left me in total amazement which I have never forgotten, and gave me a great incentive to learn more of what I had witnessed this day.

As for diversion and relaxation, I really didn't have much time. The only diversion that I really had was when in the fall and spring of each year my father, a friend of his, and me got in the Model A Ford pickup and went mushroom hunting in East Meadow and Hicksville, Long Island. Usually this would happen during rainy weekends. After I met my wife, we were really friends at the beginning, her father, my father, and the other friend would go mushroom hunting. In the summer time we would take the bus to Long Beach and Jones Beach a few times each summer to go swimming and look around.

I was given extra assignments during the sixth grade spring semester, and the teacher gave me extra tutoring on special assignments, mostly in English composition and vocabulary. When the end of the semester came in June, I was promoted to seventh grade, 1938-1939 year.

During the summer of 1938, I worked mostly with my father. When I had time to spare, with my father's help, I learned how to grow and cut flowers, and sell to people passing by. The most popular were asters, zinnias, dahlias, Japanese iris, lilies, and some roses. I'd sell a nice big bunch of flowers for twenty-five cents per bunch. With the Japanese iris I would split a large clump, about ten inches in diameter, into four sections and I would sell each section for fifty cents. Each clump or section thereof had flowers and balled roots for planting.

The land that I used belonged to a wealthy old man, Mr. West, and was attached to the back yard of our new home. He had 12 acres of uncultivated land, mostly covered with wild cherry bushes, blackberry and scrub bushes, and lots of poison ivy. One day my father asked him if I could use some of the land for flowers, and he said that as long as I cleaned it and kept clean I could use as much as I wanted. I cleaned and dug it with my father's help, and it became a flower garden that I was able to make some extra money during the summers. During this time, it was still the depression and money was still pretty scarce.

I must go back to the land that my father had bought at a tax sale in 1933. It was a corner lot in an undeveloped section of Baldwin, but which had a beautiful boulevard, built during the depression by WPA (Works Progress Administration) workers, an organization organized by President Franklin Delano Roosevelt to help the depressed unemployed people make a living through the use of federal funds. Many of these roads were built in undeveloped areas, but with fairly good planning. In this case one side of the boulevard would become flooded during storms, and the other side was 30 feet or more above the boulevard level. My father's land was on the flooding side. Since one of my father's customers was an official in the town's building department, my father asked him if he could take some dirt from the high side to fill his lot. The official told my father that he could, but he had to take the dirt from a marked area which would become a future street. One weekend he came to see my father, still living in the rental house, and told him where the markings were. In the fall of 1937 my father and I spent almost every weekend with pick and shovel, carting dirt from one side of the boulevard to the other side, the lower side. By the time the house was finished the yard was above flood level. The top of the basement walls were built three feet above flood level.

In September 1938, I began my seventh grade. Most of the school children had gotten used to us, and we had already embraced the American ways, so that we got along together very nicely. The harassing had almost stopped, and we made a great number of friends. I had to work hard to keep up with the regular seventh grade work, plus making up some missing work from the sixth grade. By the end of the first semester I was all caught up, and progressing normally with all class work and special assignments in English composition. I maintained a B average for the first semester and a B+ for the second semester (1939). I'd like to mention here that my sister followed the regular schedule and she did not skip grades like I did, so she was one year behind me. In June at the end of the semester, I was promoted to the eighth grade with a B+ average.

The summer of 1939 began as usual. I worked with my father in gardening and landscaping. One of my father's customers took me and my sister to Jones Beach for the day, and we had a nice time swimming while they watched. We were not swimmers yet, but we enjoyed the surf.

Around the middle of July 1939, a friend and countryman of my father came down to Baldwin to visit with his family- wife and two daughters- for the day. They lived in Brooklyn and came down on the Long Island Railroad. They were very nice, and while the two old friends talked about old times, the girls, my sister, and I got acquainted.

Also, across the street from us lived another countryman and his wife, and also friends of both my father and the family that came to visit. This worked very well during the visit since the two women had a great time together, gossiping and so on. The names of the family from Brooklyn were Luigi and Assunta Ventura, and the two girls were Nettie (Annette) 12 years old, and Maria, 16 years old. Nettie was very quiet while Maria was quite an extrovert, and talking a lot with my sister. At this time I was 15 years old and my sister was 17 years and very talkative. I think Nettie thought I was sort of funny because of my heavy Italian accent, and I was a little hesitant to speak much. The two of us didn't do much talking, except talking about school. I thought Nettie was small and a little knock-kneed, and to myself I called her "Little Nettie," which has stuck with me for the past 68 years, and most likely until I die. So that's how I met my future and loving wife, although at that time it wasn't even a dream yet.

The Ventura family made many more trips to Baldwin visiting us and looking for a house. The two girls and us (my sister and I) became very good and close friends, and my father helped Luigi (Louis) find an old house not too far from ours. The house needed a lot of work, and the family, especially Louis, came down weekends to restore the old house, and restore he did after six years of hard work. He bought the two-story house in 1941 for $2100 and was finished in 1945.

When the family came down, the father and mother were working mostly on their house, and after they would come and visit. While the grown-ups did their talking, my sister and Maria would fix dinner and Nettie and I would be walking in the garden and empty fields around our house and talking about school. She would tell me about the city, and the Prospect Park Museum and library, and I would tell her about the creek where we learned to swim and about the swim holes and Jones Beach.

September 1939 came and I started the 8th grade. I thought I was prepared for the 8th grade, but I took no chances; I started studying hard from the first moment I entered the classroom. The teachers were very nice and tried to be extra helpful, because of my persistent language problem, speaking-wise only. Within a week after the beginning of school, I started noticing that some of the students started to resent the extra help I was getting from my teachers. One morning I got to school extra early and I told my homeroom teacher what I thought was happening, and also told him how much I appreciated his extra help. He was very understanding and appreciative of my concern, and he told me that if and whenever I needed extra help to let him know, and he would help me in writing only. And it worked throughout the school year. He apparently passed the word to the other teachers. General Science and English were my favorite subjects in the 8ᵗʰ grade. I carried the regular schedule of subjects, plus a few additional assignments to catch up of what I had missed in the previous grades. English Composition became easier and I started to get A- and A's. The speaking part I found a little harder. Math, current events, and general sciences came quite easy. I worked very hard and intensely during my 8ᵗʰ grade.

One of the first things my father taught us when we came to America was to display the American flag during national holidays. We did so religiously, and am doing so today. We enjoyed going to the Labor Day parade, Thanksgiving parade, Columbus Day, Memorial Day, and Independence Day parades.

Come Christmas and with it came new experiences and education. In Italy there was no Christmas gift-giving or exchanging, therefore no Christmas shopping. The only time gifts were given was the day of the Epiphany, January 6ᵗʰ. Instead of a Christmas tree, we lit huge bonfires in front of our homes at exactly 6:00 PM Christmas Eve, when the church bells would ring. You could see those fires for miles, because of the hilly and mountainous landscape. The novelty of the Christmas tree, decorating the outside of the house, and exchanging of gifts was exciting and an education in itself. Of course the sight and feel of snow was another lovely excitement. We almost never had snow in the winter in Southern Italy.

In the winter, there was not much work in gardening and landscaping, so my father had somewhat of a vacation, except for occasional snow removing and garage cleaning, and therefore I had more time to read and study. This helped me a lot in doing extra assignments. When June came and school ended I was promoted to the

9th grade with a B+ average. Before I left for vacation, I asked my homeroom teacher if there was a way to accelerate my studies in high school so that I could graduate at 18 years old. He suggested I go talk to the high school principal or assistant principal, since they would be in their offices for at least one more week after school closed for the summer. That I did the following Monday. I spoke first to Miss Fuller, the assistant principal and a former Latin teacher. She was very interested in my request and a lovely and kind lady. She told me to come back next day, in the meantime she would discuss my intentions to Mr. Callister, the principal, and Mr. Newton, the Superintendent. The next day at 9:00 AM I went to the high school and there I met the three school officials in Miss Fuller's office. They had studied my record so far, had spoken to some of my former teachers, and explained to me how hard it would be for me to carry such a heavy schedule. I told them that I'd like to try if they would let me. They asked me why I wanted to do this, and I explained to them that if I followed the regular school schedule I'd be 20 years old before I would graduate. They told me they would give me a chance in the fall, on condition that I maintain a "C" or better average each semester, and for me to get in touch with them the week before school opened in the fall. In the meantime I already had my 9th grade schedule.

During the summer of 1940 I helped my father, and I worked on my odd jobs. I also had my own customers within walking distance of our home, which my father helped me get. I used the lawn mower, a Pennsylvania Quality seven blade, as a cart to carry my bushel and hand trimming tools. Several times my friends from Brooklyn came to visit, and the two girls, my sister, and I would go to either Long Beach or Jones Beach by bus. In no time at all, September came and back to school again.

As I was told by the principal and assistant principal in June, I reported to the principal's office two days before school opened and Miss Fuller, the assistant principal, had worked a schedule for me for the 9th and 10th grade. We went over it, and in order to make all the subjects fit, I would not have any study hall periods during the semester. Also if I wanted to take music as an elective, I would have to use my lunch period for it. I would be taking physical education only once a week instead of the three times a week. She also told me that I would have to attend summer school in 1941 and 1942, and that as of now, this arrangement would be on a trial basis. Should I not be able to maintain the required class level of C or better I would have to go back to the standard school routine. I told her and the principal that I would take the challenge. For the next two years I would take no extra curriculars, would not attend any sports games, no social events, and would be in class almost every day until 4:30, sometimes until 6:00 pm. Most of the teachers were wonderful and kind, especially the math, science, and social studies teachers. With their help and dedication I was able to get through the 9th and 10th grade with a class average of a B-, and in one year. However, I had to go to summer school to make up 10th grade English and trigonometry, which I did at the Freeport High School, one town away. I still managed to help my father on weekends, and sometimes late after school when the days got longer.

In June 1941, right after school closed, I asked my father if I could get a car, so that I could get to school easier and also be able to help him with his customers. I had been practicing on his Model A Ford truck by driving it back and forth in the driveway. If I got my own car then I could learn to drive in the street. My father told me that if I could find a decent car cheap that he would help me buy it. I talked to one of my classmates whose father owned an Oldsmobile dealership in Freeport if he could help me find a good cheap used car, and he said he would talk to his father. At school, before classes started, he came to talk to me, about three weeks later, that his father would allow me to go look in his used car lot and look at several cars parked along the railroad fence. He told me that his father would give me a good deal if I would choose one of these cars. The following Sunday I got on my bicycle and rode to Freeport to look at those cars. They were parked in an area along the railroad fence, covered with weeds and vines, so that I had to cut some of these vines before I could get a good look at the cars. Out of the dozen or so cars, I picked a 1935 Model 76 Oldsmobile, with an inline 6 cylinder engine that could be hand cranked if the battery was dead. It was a four door sedan with a roomy trunk, the inside was in pretty good condition, the outside was solid but oxidized and had no radio or heating. The engine was supposed to be in good running condition. The father of my classmate told me that if I bought the car he would clean it, polish it, and check the engine thoroughly. On the windshield it had a price of $250, written on the inside of the windshield with white chalk.

I went home and told my father of the price, and I also told him that I had only $100 saved from my odd jobs. The following Saturday was a very rainy day and my father couldn't work, so he took me to the car dealer, to examine the car and talk to my classmate's father about the price. It so happened that my father knew the dealer from some gardening he had done for him. After looking at the car again, with my father this time, and some negotiation, the dealer said he would sell the car to me for $190. We bought the car, and the dealer said he would deliver the car the following Saturday in the morning.

The following Saturday, a beautiful sunny spring day, a beautiful shiny black car was delivered to our house by a black man. He had a three-wheeled motorcycle hooked up in the back of the 1935 Oldsmobile, got out of the car, asked for my name and handed me the keys. He then unhooked the motorcycle and left. I was absolutely astonished by how that ugly tarnished car turned out so beautiful. I studied the dashboard, the floor shifting lever, the brakes, clutch, and gas pedal, and sat in the driver's seat and started the car. It was much easier than my father's Model A pick up; no magneto lever, no timing levers and best of all no manual choke.

Since I had arrived in the United States, I had developed an interest in automobiles and all their intricacies, especially the engine. After I had learned the English language, around the beginning of 1938, I would run to the old Baldwin library whenever I had some spare time, and read Audel's auto mechanic books. Whenever I passed a gas station I would stop and watch the mechanic work, and sometimes ask questions on what he was doing, and almost always got an answer.

In the spring of 1940, I decided that I wanted to learn about car engines in my little spare time I had. So near the junction of Milburn Avenue and Sunrise Highway was Terry's junkyard, with dozens of wrecked and junked cars lying exposed to the weather. One day coming home from school, I took a slight detour to Terry's junkyard, and asked him if he had an old beat-up motor that I could buy cheap. He asked my name and I gave it to him, and then told me that he knew my father. He also asked me why I wanted an old engine, and I told him that I wanted to take it apart and put it together to learn how it worked and how it was put together. He asked how much money I had and told him I didn't have any, but that I had a few lawns and odd jobs to do during the weekend and I would come back. He said all right, and he would look for a cheapie. When I got home I told my father about it, and he told me that as long as I got all my school work done, I could have the engine, and showed me where to put it in the backyard.

I went back to the junkyard two weeks later, on a weekend. Terry was busy taking a car apart, told me to wait, that he would be with me in half an hour and that I could look around if I wanted to. I told him that I'd rather watch him instead and he said ok. When he finished, he showed me a whole pile of engines in a muddy patch of dirt. I picked one which looked pretty beat up but had all the parts. He told me that it was an oil burner, and had no compression, and that I could have it for five dollars. I told him I only had $3.75, and after thinking for a few minutes he told me I could have it, and on his way home he would drop it off in our backyard. He asked me if I had tools and I told him I didn't. He advised me that when I had a few dollars for me to go to the Strauss auto discount store, and there I could get some good tools real cheap. I told my father about my project and asked if it would be alright for me to buy some tools with the next five dollars instead of depositing it in my savings account, and he approved.

Within two weeks I had made a little more than six dollars at odd jobs, and my father took me to the Strauss store to buy some tools. I bought a hand socket set with a six inch "L" shaped handle, a set of box wrenches and a 12 oz hammer, all for seven dollars. My father helped a little. With the help of the library and the Audel's auto mechanic books, I took that engine apart and put it back together in less than three months, and had no parts left over. The Audel's auto mechanic book taught me more than taking an engine apart. I learned about carburetors, chokes, brakes, lights and the electrical system of a car. So that when I bought my first car the next year, I was not totally ignorant about its workings.

By the way, I got rid of that engine by asking Terry the junk owner if he would take it back, and he did with a smile.

Come September 1941, I started my 11th and 12th grade in high school. During the summer of 1941 I went to Freeport High School to finish my 10th grade subjects. It was an accelerated semester of six weeks, but it was worth it.

My assistant principal had outlined a program for me, and asked me to go to her office with some of my teachers and discuss it the day before school opened. We sat down and I went over the whole program for the two grades, and it was approved with the condition that I maintain a minimum average of a "C" in every subject. Also I would have to go to summer school in 1942 to complete English 12. I could take orchestra and Glee Club as extracurricular subjects during lunch only. I ate lunch between class changes. It was a hard year. At times I thought of giving up but I persisted, and ended up with an overall average of B- for the fall and spring semesters. Although my father was not an educated man he supported me all the way. While going to school, I attended no social or party events of any kind in school. However, I did see My Little Nettie several times when the family came down from the city, and after I got the car we would go to Jones Beach on Sunday with my sister, her sister, and a few times her cousins. In the summer of 1942, her cousins from New Jersey came down to Baldwin to visit and we all went to Jones Beach one Saturday.

1942 - High School graduation
Photo— 18 years old

Our Family home,-11 Eastern Blvd.,
Baldwin, L.I.,N. 1942.

1941 - My first car,-1935
Oldsmobile, model 76.

1941

In the summer of 1942, I completed my 12th year English, but I still needed two electives required for graduation. In September I registered for the two electives and two advanced math classes, required for college entrance curriculum. This was a light schedule compared to the previous years. I was carrying B+ and A's during the 1942 semester, but WWII was getting mighty serious, and sooner than later, I would be drafted. I wanted to get into aviation rather than be drafted into the regular army. So the first week of November 1942, I informed the assistant principal that I intended to volunteer into the US Army Air Corps before I'd get drafted, and if it would be possible for me to take the final exams on my subjects before I enlisted. She told me that she would look into it and let me know within a few days.

The following Monday I was called in the principal's office and was told that the final exams would be ready for me to take on the 16th and 17th of November. I took the last two exams on Friday, November 17th, and on Monday, November 20th I went to the Commodore Hotel in New York City at 8:00 AM to enlist in the United States Army Air Corps. It was an all day affair. First having a physical, then oral tests, psychological tests, eye and ear tests, and all the rest. I had with me three letters of recommendation from my assistant principal, principal, and superintendent of Baldwin High School, and after my physical I handed them to the officer who was giving the oral tests. At about 4:30 in the afternoon they handed me two sheets of paper. On the first sheet it said "accepted US Army Air Corps" and the second had instructions for me to report for duty on the 27th of November at 7:30 AM, at Camp Upton, Yaphank, Long Island, New York.

During those last days, I was busy putting things away for the duration of the war, and storing my car until I came back, if I did come back. I did not have a chance to say goodbye to Little Nettie, but I had said goodbye to her father the previous Sunday. I really never told her that, to myself, I called her Little Nettie, until 68 years later, although I had her in my prayers since I was 18 years old, and still do. I also helped my father move some heavy items in the back yard and around the house, and straightened the tools in the garage before I left.

The Military

On November 27th, 1942, I got up at 4:30 AM, as did my father and sister, had a nice breakfast together, packed my shaving items in a small bag, and got ready to be driven by my father to Camp Upton. Our Italian friend, Joe Scorzo, who lived across the street also got up early to come and keep my father company. At 5:30 AM, I kissed and hugged my sister, and left for Camp Upton in the Model A Ford pick up to make the 65 miles by 7:30.

During these days there were no expressways or turnpikes, so travel was all by local roads and slow. We took Sunrise Highway all the way to Patchogue, then northeast on a small county road until we came by the back gate of Camp Upton. An MP (military patrol) met us, asked for acceptance documents, and told me to say goodbye to my father. I hugged and kissed my father, as he told me to always follow orders and be a good soldier. I said goodbye to the Italian friend, hugged my father again, and with teary eyes we parted and I walked through the gate, where an army bus was waiting with half a dozen other inductees.

We drove for about one mile, where temporary warehouses and barracks had been erected, and dozens of new inductees were already in line. We got off the bus and got in the back of the line. A noncommissioned officer came by with a clipboard and pen in hand, writing down everybody's names and checking the induction papers, and writing down our social security number, religious denomination, next of kin, and our blood type if we knew it. For those of us who did not know our blood type, we were lined up separately. Next we were told to line up for clothing in a long corridor of the barrack. We each were given a complete change of clothes. This included one set of underwear, socks, boots, shirt, a fatigue hat, a pair of fatigue coveralls, handkerchief, a field jacket and a pair of gloves- all in military, olive drab colors. Then we were given a cardboard box, and told to take of all the clothes we had on, pack them in the box, and write our family address on it, and put on the issued clothes. As soon as we were dressed in the new wardrobe, we were lined up in a long line and told to march through a large open door in an adjacent barrack. As we marched, permanent party soldiers outside kept yelling at us "the hook, watch out for the hook." Most of us had no idea of what they were saying, but soon found out. As we entered the large open door, on the inside were six medics, three on each side as we entered, with multi-dosage syringes. Hence the hook! We were ordered to roll up our sleeves on each side, and as we walked through the narrow gate we were given six injections- typhoid, diphtheria, and God knows what else. Some of the new inductees passed out when they saw the needles, some cried, and some cursed!

The line which had all those who didn't have a blood type, were directed into another door where medics pricked our fingers to take a sample of blood. Then all the inductees, now recruits, were marched to a nearby warehouse, where each one of us was issued a working tool. These were axes, hoes, picks, handsaws, and crowbars and told to line up outside, where a staff sergeant was waiting for us. He was in charge of us and we were to obey him in every way. My tool of choice was a five inch bladed axe.

I must mention here, that it was the end of November and it gets very cold and windy on Long Island. Thank God that the issued underwear was all winter wear, and the field jacket was a fairly good windbreaker, or we would have frozen. Anyway, the staff sergeant lined us up in three parallel lines, and marched us to a field of intense scrub pines, showed us a patch about 45 feet by 65 feet, marked by red stakes, and told us to clear it, level it, and clean it because that's where we would be sleeping tonight. This had to be completed by 4:00 PM, erect a 20 feet by 40 feet tent for us to live in. Then he told us to start working now and dismissed us from formation.

While many of the inductees, recruits now, were trying to figure out what to do with and how to use the tools they were issued, I went to work with my axe. In less than one hour I had chopped down around 20 or 25 trees, and going strong, because I wanted to prevent my arms from becoming sore from the injections. After about one hour the staff sergeant, around forty-five years old, came to me and said, "Where did you come from?" and I answered, "From home." He chuckled and told me to carry on.

At 12:00 noon we were assembled, lined up as before, and marched to rest rooms and the mess hall (dining barrack) for lunch. We had approximately 45 minutes for lunch. We lined up before the food counters, they had trays at the beginning of the line, and in no time we were served and eating. Before we knew the whistle blew for us to line-up, as we did, the staff sergeant told us we had five minutes to go to the rest room, and line up to go back to clearing our future living area. The sergeant had six permanent party soldiers with him to help with this task. Their job was to push the less enthusiastic recruits to do their job, and to keep an orderly working atmosphere. Needless to say, the job was completed before the deadline, and trucks with the materials for setting up a 20 feet by 40 feet tent were waiting on site.

At 4:00 in the afternoon we were lined up in formation, and marched to the supply barracks once more, this time to get our full issue of clothes and bedding. This time we got our winter dress uniform, two sets of underwear, two fatigue coveralls, two pairs of boots, four pairs of socks, handkerchiefs, two pairs of pants, two shirts, one necktie, dog tags, a GI (government issue) belt with brass buckles, a mess kit, canteen with cup, and bedding and towels. Bedding included two GI blankets, 2 sheets, pillow and pillow cases. Also we got two dress hats, one khaki, and one OD (to match our winter uniform), and of course one fatigue hat. Also we were issued one duffle bag to keep our possessions in. The next morning we had our duffle bags stenciled with our name and permanent ID number. While we went to supper, we parked our new possessions in an empty barrack near the mess all, since our living quarters were not yet ready.

After supper we picked up our new issues and walked to our newly installed tent on the land that we had cleared during the afternoon. The permanent party soldiers had two 20 feet by 40 feet tents side by side installed next to each other, each with approximately 30 cots and three pot belly stoves.

The next day we were awakened at 5:00 AM, told to dress up and get to the toilets and washrooms approximately 300 feet from our tents, clean up, shave and be back at the tents in 30 minutes. After that was accomplished we were marched to the mess hall (dining area, that is), given 15 minutes for washing up and restrooms, and then we marched to a huge amphitheater. All the chairs had a writing arm to it. This was test time. All morning we took tests of all kinds. Later I was told that it was an IQ test. After lunch we had more tests, mostly aptitude tests. On the third day it was physical examination time. Each one of us was examined from head to toe, and even more blood tests were done.

The fourth and fifth day was the beginning of training, learning the ins and outs of marching, different maneuvers, indoctrination in military rules and regulations, and we were told to study our military manual. We spent all our time outside even though it was cold and windy, and we ate from a field kitchen, where all the food was prepared and eaten outside. All the cooking was done on open fire pits outside, and for the first time we learned the meaning and use of the mess kit and canteen cup. The sixth day was results and decisions day. The number of recruits applying for the army air corps were separated from all the rest of the inductees, approximately 500 men. We were lined up in this large open area in front of the administration headquarters and our names were called one by one by two non-commissioned officers. As our name was called we stepped forward and each one marched to an area about 30 feet away. The army was separating those recruits who had an IQ of 110 and above from those who scored lower. Out of the 500 or so recruits only 300 had a score of 110 and higher. The rest of the recruits who had lower scores were sent for reclassification. The 300 selected were to go, the next day, to Miami Beach for six weeks of testing and basic training.

On the 7th day again we were awakened at 5:00 AM and after breakfast we were lined up and marched in front of headquarters, all 300 of us who were going to Miami Beach. An officer explained to us that we were going on a troop train, and that they were asking for volunteers to work on the train while en route. I volunteered, because I didn't like the idea of just sitting for three or four days. After they got the needed number of volunteers, we marched about half a mile and boarded a troop train, surrounded by MP (Military Patrols). As soon as we boarded the names of those who volunteered for duty were called, and were assigned duties to perform during the trip. I was assigned to KP (kitchen duty) for the duration of the trip. I was assigned to making salads and serving food, which I thought was pretty good, although it got me quite tired by the end of the day.

After we arrived at Miami Beach we were marched to our living quarters. I was assigned to a room at the Majestic Hotel, located on Ocean Drive and 8th Street. It was a simple building with no air conditioning during these days, and shared toilets. It took us three days to get to Miami Beach, with many stops and side tracking to avoid the 5th column threat (sabotage threat).

As soon as we arrived we went through the basics of basic training, and were shown many health related films emphasizing the dangers of venereal diseases. Also we were shown films on security, and military intelligence, especially about not discussing military activities outside of the military arena. After one and one half days of orientation we began the real basic training. We were issued rifles, mostly WWI infields models, without ammunition. After supper we were given less than one hour to rest and then were marched to theaters for more testing. Some was multiple choices, then we had mathematics problems and in at least three testing sections we had to write essays of at least 500 words or more. We had to take mechanical and radio code aptitude tests, whereby we had to listen to morse code and to distinguish the difference between sounds.

Once all the testing was accomplished we had continuous basic training. Marching maneuvers, parading, rifle and pistol range, personal defense and learning to dig fox holes. Also learning about field hygiene. We also had to perform M.P. guard patrol, and of course K.P. We all had to take at least one turn at each one. One thing I forgot to mention is that every day we were in the army air corps, we had forty-five minutes of calisthenics, rain or shine, even at school.

Having completed basic training sometime in January 1943, we were marched to the railroad station to board a Pullman train for somewhere. Of the approximately 300 recruits that came to Miami

Beach from Camp Upton, only about half made the grade for technical command schools. So, the approximately 150 soldiers who made the grade boarded the Pullman, dressed in khaki summer wear. By late afternoon we left Miami Beach, with our assumption that we were headed for either Texas or California. Instead four days later we arrived in Sioux falls, South Dakota in a blizzard with outside temperatures of -20 degrees F. We were still dressed in summer wear. Because of the danger of sabotage the train had zig-zagged all about the central US before arriving to Sioux Falls.

The train coasted right against a huge warehouse alongside tracks, and we were ordered to disembark from the train and go into that warehouse- a walk of approximately 35-40 feet in that below-zero weather. Twenty soldiers got pneumonia, and several of us got arthritis in the legs and arm joints. I got it in my knees, and was hospitalized for five days. Once in the heated warehouse we all were told to change into our OD's or winter clothes and wear our winter coats. Two of the soldiers who got pneumonia died, and all the rest of us recovered after one week in the army hospital. After two days of therapeutic and medicinal treatments those who could walk around were given chores helping those patients more seriously ill.

The moment we left the hospital we were assigned to barracks and marched to Morse code classes, to learn Morse code and messaging. The duration of this training was officially twelve weeks, or until the students learned to receive a minimum of 16 words per minute. Those students who achieved the 16 words per minute in shorter time were transferred to advanced radio operator classes, and/or aerial gunnery school if they had requested it and qualified. Those of us who had been accepted into the radio mechanic field were sent to Truax Field, Madison, Wisconsin for radio mechanic training for 12 weeks.

While in basic training in Miami Beach, and Morse code training in Sioux Falls, My Little Nettie and I corresponded frequently. She wrote very sweet friendly letters and I did the same although I wanted to write more affectionate letters to her. I didn't because I was afraid I'd offend her. I loved and waited for her letters, even though we signed them with an "I miss you." This correspondence continued until I came home after the war.

At the command school in Sioux Falls, I learned to receive and send the 16 words per minute before the twelve weeks were over, but continued attending classes until we were shipped out to Truax Field, Madison, Wisconsin for radio mechanic training. We rose at 5:00 am, cleaned up, dressed up in the uniform of the day, went to breakfast, and then one hour of calisthenics and marching. When we returned we had a fifteen minute rest to wash up, dress in fatigues, and march to classes. Classes were held five and one half days per week, on rotating shifts. Some weeks I was on the first shift, then second shift and then on the third or "graveyard shift." The classes were 8 hours long, and besides classes we also had military training, such as learning to fire all types of weapons, target practice on the firing range, and learning safety tactics. Saturday afternoon we usually got passes to go to town, and return Sunday night by 8:00 pm. Bed check was at 9:30 pm.

The local farmers and canning factories asked the camp headquarters for help, and asked for volunteers on their time off to help them pick crops or help in the canning factories, days or nights. I volunteered and spent most of my time off on weekends helping in the canning of string beans and corn. We didn't get any pay, but plenty of good food and all the beer or soft drinks we could drink. I didn't drink beer but had plenty of soft drinks and coffee. A few times me and three of my buddies went roller skating at the University of Wisconsin. When we arrived at Truax Field in Madison, the weather was terribly cold, windy, and wet, and by the time we completed our training, flowers were popping out of the ground. All the while I had been in the Service so far, I kept getting letters from my high school friends and many of my former teachers, and of course very frequently from My Little Nettie, while I waited with anticipation every week. Also while training, on two weekends I participated in skits or plays we gave for the rest of the troops. In one play I was the efficiency expert in a beer factory, and in the other I was the "belle of the ball" in a shady bar. For the effort the company commander gave all the participants a three-day pass to Chicago with all transportation paid, on the luxury train express called the Hiawatha Express from St. Paul, Minnesota to Chicago.

I didn't know anything about Chicago, so I took a trolley from the train directly to the Serviceman Center, and registered there so I'd have a place to stay and sleep. They were very helpful, mostly volunteers, and they told me about all the activities going on, including at the service center. All the activities were hosted by volunteers. They had a canteen were they served food and drinks, playing cards, a booth where you could listen to phonograph records, and a dancing area with music provided by a juke box, and many volunteer women and girls to dance with. I listened to records for a while, then I went to the dancing area, got me a coca cola and watched the servicemen and their partners dance. While sitting down sipping my coke, this lady came over and asked me why I was not on the dancing floor. I told her I didn't know how to dance, and she asked me if I wanted something to eat. It was past 5 o'clock in the afternoon, and I said yes and that maybe I'd go get a hamburger. She said she would go with me and that we could eat together. She asked me what nationality I was from because of my accent, and asked if she could teach me how to dance. I told her that the only dances I knew were the waltz, the tarantella, the mazurka, and the polka, none of which were going on the floor. Then she told me that her shift was almost over, and invited me to her house, a block away from the service center, to have coffee and cake. I was afraid to say yes, but then I thought that if I said no it would be impolite and possibly hurt her feelings. So I said yes. We walked about one and a half blocks to an all-brick tenement house, more like an old apartment house. She opened the door into a very nice apartment. She asked me to sit down and that she would make coffee. Next to where I was sitting was a side table with a picture of a young man in a sailor suit. In a few minutes she brought me a cup of coffee, and I asked her if the fellow in the picture was her husband, and she told me that it was her 18-year-old son. She told me that she was going to change into something more comfortable and then we would have cake. She returned after five minutes, in a see-through negligee with nothing underneath. With all my 19 years of urges and desires I told her I had to leave because my buddies and I had planned some excursion early next morning, and I left, feeling sorry for her. My thoughts of what my mother had taught me, and the thought of Little Nettie, would not permit me to do otherwise. And never did otherwise until after I was married.

Upon completing our training at Truax Field, we were sent to Wisconsin Rapids for field training, such as guard duty and security, laying field communication lines, and survival. We lived in open fields and tents, cooked and ate from field kitchens, and did field maneuvers.

Upon completion of this training we were shipped to Tomah, Wisconsin for the final leg of our command school training. It was an American Indian college taken over by the U.S. Army forces for training in intelligence-related work. Here we trained for C.N.S (Control Net System) which was basically the predecessor of today's air control system. This was performed by triangulation, in the field by using three directional finding units located between 12 and 20 miles apart, in a triangular pattern. Each unit taking a coordinate fix on a flying craft, relaying the information to a control center several miles away, which would plot the three readings, and thus giving the exact location of the flying aircraft. All this to be performed in approximately 1.5 minutes. All the schooling in Tomah was secret, so that when we went to class we could not have pencils, paper, or any kind of notepads. We had to memorize all the information taught to us.

Out of the 150 or so soldiers that started this course, only 100 graduated. This was only my group. There were also four other groups which attended the same training at Truax Field. The total graduation form Truax Field including all five groups was 425 students. Approximately 150 were selected to go to Tomah for C.N.S. training, and approximately 100 graduated.

After graduating from Tomah, we were shipped out in different directions for further war training. I was shipped out to Hammer Field, California for six weeks of desert combat training. This was around early October 1943. I was the only one selected to go for desert combat training from my class.

My orders and travel papers were cut and the next morning I was on my way to Hammers Field. The train took me to Fresno, California where I was met by an MP and ordered to board an army 6x6 truck for the trip to Hammer Field, some 20 or 30 miles south-east of Fresno. Around 8 or 10 more soldiers were in the truck with me. The base was set up or built next to the Italian Swiss Colony Winery-in a sandy area with hundreds of four-bed tents. We were issued combat gear- uniforms, a springfield rifle, ammunition, and a light machine gun. The gear was marked with each soldier's permanent ID number and loaded into trucks. The next day, early in the morning, we were called to order, and after breakfast, with canteens full of water we started the march to Mt. Owens in the Mojave Desert. They had set up water stations and an ambulance every 6 or 8 miles along the way, where we also had rest stops, although we were given a 10 minute rest break every two hours. The temperature in the sun was between 80 and 90 degrees F. all the way. We arrived in a tent area in the desert just as it was getting dark. We were told to line up, ordered to attention, then at ease while they did roll call.

After roll call my name and another soldier by the name of Ames were called and asked to step forward. We were told that during the next six weeks we were to man the orderly tent for the squadron. And so we did, in addition to the combat training. This included keeping records for all the personnel in training, typing and posting orders and bulletins, and keeping track of any medical and sick calls. Also ordering supplies and equipment from quartermaster headquarters, and of course reveille every morning. Every Saturday, we updated all the records. The only benefit out of this duty was that the two of us didn't have to attend or participate in parades, or fall out for formations, for the purpose of inspections. Every other phase of the combat training we had to do just like the soldiers, including simulated attacks and counterattacks, infiltration courses, and firing range using rifles, side arms, and hand-held machine guns. Also we had to go through the hand grenade throwing exercises.

At the completion of the training in the desert, we packed our gear, guns, and everything else, and loaded them on trucks. The orderly tent supplies, equipment, and record files we loaded in a special truck, and me and Ames were allowed to ride back to Hammer Field, instead of marching back. While still in California, we had Christmas 1943 in a sandy, out-of-the-way place in south California, being entertained by Eddy Cantor and Alan Hale sr. I can't remember too much about it.

Two days after returning to Hammerfield, I was told of a four-day furlough, en-route to my next assignment, to a P-39 Airdrome in Redding, California. The traveling papers were cut to New York by way of Chicago, on the Union Pacific Railroad. Spend my furlough in Baldwin, Long Island. At the end of my four-day furlough, travel to Chicago, re-group with my C.N.S group, and travel to Redding California by troop train. This must have been early January 1944.

After three days and tree nights on the Union Pacific Railroad, I arrived in Chicago, in old oil lamp lit rail cars. In Chicago I boarded the Pennsylvania Railroad to New York and Baldwin, Long Island, to my father and sister Giulia. It was early afternoon when I got home, kissed and hugged my father and sister, and I called Little Nettie in Brooklyn. She was very happy that I called, and asked me if my sister and I would like to go to Radio City to see the Christmas show that was still playing. I said yes.

On my second day home, in the morning, my sister and I boarded the Long Island Railroad train and went to Brooklyn. I was greeted warmly by the family and very warmly by Little Nettie and her sister Maria. As we left the house for Radio City Music Hall, Little Nettie's mother told us to come back to their house for dinner after the show. The four of us left for the trolley car that took us to the subway that brought us to Radio City Music Hall. We had a very short wait in line to get tickets and proceeded inside. Me and my sister had never been at Radio City before, and we marveled at its beauty. We sat somewhere near the center of the theater, me and Little Nettie together, between my sister and her sister.

The Christmas show and the Rockettes were wonderful and we really enjoyed it very much. Then came the main feature, "Cover Girl," with Rita Hayworth and Gene Kelly. I was so happy and excited to be sitting next to Little Nettie, but I tried not to show it, because I was afraid she might get offended. However, I tried to get closer and she didn't seem to mind. While Rita Hayworth was singing "Long Ago and Far Away," I put my arm over her shoulder and she didn't react negatively. I had my arm around her for the rest of the show. Her sister smiled and my sister said nothing. It was a memorable day for me, and years later my wife told me it was the same for her.

After the show we returned to Little Nettie's house, and her mother had prepared a wonderful dinner for us that we enjoyed very much. Afterwards, we sat down and after we went over the events of the day, we left for the railroad station accompanied by Little Nettie and Maria. As the train approached, we said goodbye and shook hands, with the hope of seeing each other soon. It would be two years before that would happen.

I spent one more day home with my father and sister, and on the following morning I took a train to Chicago to rendezvous with C.N.S. Trained Troops, for a troop train to California. Upon arrival at the Chicago Station we reported to the M.P. desk, and were herded into a waiting troop train. Actually it wasn't a really troop train because the front cars were for nonmilitary passengers. After about two days we arrived at Ogden, Utah, where we were told there would be a five-hour stop over and we could get off the train, and could go to eat or shop. Ogden was located in a valley surrounded by mountains, and was very cold with snow on the ground.

I and two of my buddies were hungry and decided to explore the local eatery. Near the railroad station we saw a diner, with several horses tied at a railing in front and we decided to go in. Inside we were greeted by five or six cowboys seated at the counter. They told us that the chili bowl was the best choice in town, and that if we'd order it they would treat us. I never had chili con carne before so I told my buddies that I would try it, and they did the same. Before we started eating one of the cowboys told us to order a large beer or a very large glass of water, and we did as suggested. As we started eating, I heard one big whelp from my buddies and as I started eating I knew why. I was used to spicy and hot food, but my buddies weren't. The chili con carne was super hot, but delicious. Regardless, we asked for more bread and finished our bowls of chili and the cowboys patted us on the back as they paid for us. I thought it was a beautiful gesture by those cowboys to treat us.

The next stop was Sacramento, California, where we got off the train, lined up and were split into several groups. My group of approximately 12 or 16 men were given orders to board a train for Redding, California. The other groups were similarly ordered to board trains for other training stations. When we got to Redding, a 6x6 army truck was waiting to cart us to the airdrome, located along the edge of a river. It was pouring rain when we arrived in California, and the river bank was riding pretty high, which sort of intimidated us somewhat.

There were four barracks on raised cement block base. One barrack was for enlisted men, one for officers, one was kitchen and mess hall, and the fourth was the day room and recreation barrack. The one runway and associated building were above the barracks about 20 or 30 feet, and the control tower was a high booth located halfway between the ends of the runway. About 15 or 20 P-39 Aircobra fighter planes were parked along one end of the runway near the buildings.

Next morning, after breakfast and calisthenics, we were given orders and instructions in setting up the three stations, directional finding stations. First we got in 3 jeeps, 5 soldiers in each, and headed out to find three locations for setting up the stations. These locations had to be at least five miles apart in a triangular configuration. That accomplished, we returned to base, reported our findings, and we were assigned the equipment to use: one enclosed van on a 6x6 truck frame with the required electronic equipment, and one gasoline operated generator mounted on a trailer for supplying the power required to operate each station. The 16th soldier of our group was the recording clerk, in charge of keeping and maintaining a complete and accurate record of all activities and operations. We repeated this operation several times by relocating our stations farther apart, as far as 20 miles apart.

The young pilots worked with us very efficiently. They would go up in different directions, we would pick up their signals, the control room would plot our readings and locate the flying aircraft fairly accurately about 60% of the times. After about one month we were proficient and accurate in about 95% of the times.

At this time we received orders to move on to Ontario, California for more advanced training both in directional finding, homing stations, and on-aircraft radio equipment maintenance, tuning and installing. In the meantime I kept receiving and writing letters from and to Little Nettie, sometimes twice weekly and sometimes every two weeks. At this time just friendly letters.

At Ontario air base we were assigned to train with P-38 "Lightening" fighter squadrons. If I remember correctly, two squadrons of P-38's flown by young pilots just out of advanced flight training. This afforded a two-way training effort. Pilots in sending distress signals and us receiving, tracking, plotting, and relaying their position back. The system was similar to that at Redding, except for the addition of a homing station at the end of the runway, and a fully-qualified control room at the air base, just as it would be in a real combat area. The homing station was similar to a direction-finding station with capabilities to guide a pilot into the runway for landing.

Our stations were located in vineyards and orange groves in Ontario, Pomona and Riverside. During the day we would work and train with the CNS system, during the night from 6:00 pm to 11:00 pm we would go into the p-38's, and check all their communication sets; tune them, test them, and if necessary replace them with good working units. One special unit, the SCR-522 Liaison Set, was of most interest to us because through this unit, all the direction-finding signals were transmitted and received. After completion of our training at Ontario Airbase, we were ready to be shipped overseas. Within two days we were given individual travel papers with a 3-day en-route pass to visit our families, before reporting to Greensboro, North Carolina, overseas processing center.

I arrived home to my father and sister in four and a half days later. Actually gave me two day's furlough after discounting local travel time. Little Nettie was in school, and I didn't have time to go to Brooklyn to see her, but I said goodbye on the phone. I spent the time with my father and sister, who tried to spoil me for these two days. My father, having been in World War One himself, understood what would be ahead, but didn't say anything, other than to tell me to take care, be good, and write as often as you can and don't forget God.

I'd like to mention here that my tour in Ontario was fairly interesting. One weekend a group of us GI's (Government Issue) or soldiers were guests of Charles Couburn (theater), treated like VP's. We were served dinner in his house by actors and actresses, including Ann Miller, Red Skeleton, Peggy Ryan, and many others that I can't remember. Red Skeleton and Ann Miller were two of the entertainers. Also in staggered groups we were taken to Hollywood for a day, where we took in the sights such as Griffen Park observatory, the Brown Derby, and the USO where Martha Ray was entertaining. We met Lou Costello and his partner Abbot, whereby they invited us to the Brown Derby. We went in the Brown Derby and soon found out that the treat was on us, and we ran out as soon as we found out that a nickel coke cost one dollar. One week-end the special services of the army took the same group of us to see the play "Abe's Irish Rose," in downtown Los Angeles.

Now back to traveling to Greensboro. On the third day of my furlough in the morning I said goodbye to my father and sister, went to the railroad station, and boarded a train for Pennsylvania Station, in New York. In New York I waited more than one hour before I boarded a train to Washington, DC. The train was jammed with people, both military and civilian; there wasn't a seat to be had in the car I was in. With my duffle bag in hand I went to the next car, and it was full. So I stopped near the door of the coach and stood there, when a woman's voice said to me, "I think we can make room for you here," as they moved closer together. They were two Navy officers, nurses I presumed, because both had the rank of Lieutenant Commander. I sat down and the woman closer to me asked what branch of the army I was in. I told her the Air Corps, and she asked me where I was going. We didn't say anything else, but since I was very tired I fell asleep, and when I woke up, just before we reached Washington, I was leaning on her shoulder. I was so very much embarrassed and I apologized, and before I got off the train she gave me a smile and wished me good luck. I wished her the same and thanked her. After I got off the train, I approached an MP and asked where I could get a train for Greensboro. He pointed to a line of maybe 100-150 soldiers and told me to get in line. In about one hour a train, made up of old rail coaches, arrived at the platform which we were lined up and were ordered to board it. Several MP's and a couple of officers were leading us into which car to get in by calling out names one by one. After about one half hour on the track we started moving. Several hours later we stopped, and we saw from the windows of the train a long line of parked military busses. We arrived at this base, with hundreds of temporary barrack, just before dark. We were marched into a huge warehouse, told to lay down our duffle bags, were given 15 minutes to get washed up and use the restrooms, and then marched to a huge mess hall to have supper. We had arrived at Greensboro processing center, sometime in mid or late April 1944. After supper we were marched to our barracks in groups of about 60 soldiers to each barrack and assigned to bunk beds. Finally we got some rest, and I came to realize how fond I was of Little Nettie and how I missed her. I wrote her a letter but didn't tell her how I felt about her. I was going overseas and had no idea what was in store for me for the future.

The first couple of days at Greensboro we all were assigned to different details. I was assigned to KP the first day, where I had to peel potatoes, bushels of them, but did them by machine. The first time I saw a potato peeling machine. It was like a tumbling machine more like a small concrete mixer, with the inside lined with either rough emery cloth or coarse sandpaper. It did the job pretty well and fast, like a bushel in less than ten minutes. The second day I was on guard duty, and after that physical examinations, and a few more tests. They found that I had compacted wisdom teeth and ordered them pulled before shipping for overseas. They were so hard to pull that after they chipped away I landed in the hospital for 3 days, the army base hospital that is. I must have spent more than one week there. Two days before we shipped out we were taken to Greensboro in army busses for last minute shopping to the largest general store that I had seen. The town seemed to be about 5 or 6 buildings, two bars, a barber shop, and the largest general store, which also had a pharmacy attached to it, and the post office. We were in town about one hour, and then another group came and we went back to camp. This continued all day long. The camp also had a large PX (Post Exchange) but no matter what time of day you went it was always jammed with soldiers. The last day every soldier was checked for VD (venereal diseases) and late in the evening we boarded a troop train for Newport News, to board a troop ship for overseas.

We arrived at Newport News early next morning. As we got off the train we were marched to a large mess hall for breakfast (chow) and use of restrooms (latrines). After chow we fell in formation, marched to a briefing area near the docks and we thoroughly were informed on what to expect and act on board ship, but we were not told where we were going. The ship was the S.S. General Randall, and this would be its maiden voyage. On board would be 6600 troops and related personnel such as nurses, crew, and marine guards. A coast guard crew would man the bridge. The ship had two 5-inch guns, one mounted on the bow and the other aft. This would be our defense against Japanese or other hostile crafts.

At approximately 10:00 am, troops started boarding the ship. My group, Army Air Corps, was one of the first groups to board. As we boarded, at the entrance was a desk with an officer recruiting volunteers to help with ship chores and details. I didn't want to spend the trip in a crowded hold, so I asked the officer where to sign. An army clerk took my name, serial number, and the information from the card given to me as I entered the ship. The card contained my name, hold and bunk number assigned to me. The officer told me to bring my gear to my assigned location, and then report to the ships galley on the double. Because we were one of the first to board, our hold was the lowest on the ship, water line. I parked my duffle bag and helmet on my assigned bunk, tied the ID tag to the frame, and rushed upstairs to the galley, deck level.

Once in the galley, I found myself with at least another dozen of GI's (soldiers) facing an army tech sergeant and a coast guard non-commissioned officer (NCO), asking my name and army serial number. We were told that we'd be assigned to details alphabetically, and to the most important details first. Me being "A," I was assigned to KP with at least eight more men. The tech sergeant was an Army Cook, and put us to work at once in preparing the evening meal for all the troops. At the same time we found out that the ship's crew consisted of one-third permanent coast guard and two-thirds volunteers- this included kitchen personnel, gun crew, repair and maintenance, and deck maintenance. The benefits from all this, we'd get three meals a day, and had to report to the hold only once in the morning for roll call. If we were on shift rotation we didn't even have to do that.

By 4:00 in the afternoon all troops and personnel were aboard, and prepared for castoff. The ship headed east and we were sure that we were headed for Africa or Europe.

We traveled east in the Atlantic Ocean until around 8:00 the next morning, when all of a sudden the ship made a 180 degree turn and headed westward. We were told by the coastguard NCO that the captain had to travel 500 miles into the Atlantic before he opened his travel orders. In about one day of traveling westward we arrived at the mouth of the Panama Canal.

The day before we left Greensboro, a bulletin was posted in all the barracks to the effect that all correspondence out had to be mailed by 6:00 pm that evening. I wrote a letter to my father and sister, and one to Little Nettie stating how much I enjoyed going to Radio City with her, and that I was fond of her. Also mentioned in the letters that it might be a long time before I would receive mail, but as long as the mail would be addressed to the APO I gave them, I would eventually receive it.

We crossed the Panama Canal during the day. It was muggy, hot, and full of mosquitoes on deck, and being waved at by the American soldiers stationed along the canal. We traveled along the coast of South America to avoid Japanese submarines, since we had no escorts. However, on the third day out of the Panama Canal the scanner crew on the bridge spotted a submarine following us at a distance, and the gun crews ran for the five-inch guns. The guns were manned by coastguard personnel, supported by GI volunteers. Whenever the spotters and radar (primitive at that time) noticed the periscope or the submarine tried to surface the gun crews fired, keeping the submarine underwater. The idea was that as long as the submarine was underwater, it could not come within range of our ship. The sub underwater could not go faster than 12 to 16 miles per hour. We were followed for two days, and then the submarine disappeared.

Halfway to the equator one of the two propeller shafts on our ship cracked, and had to travel on one propeller for one and a half days while the crew welded the broken shaft together. That accomplished we proceeded at cruising speed once again. Within 3 or 4 days we approached the equator, and preparation for the crossing ceremonies got underway. Most of the KP volunteers were rotated as to jobs on the ship. I was assigned to deck and gun maintenance and upkeep under a coastguard NCO. One of our jobs was to set up a PA (Public Announcement) system on the aft deck for the equator crossing ceremonies. I was assigned that task under the guidance of a coast guard electrician. It took us one whole day to do the set up and probably a half mile of electrical wire. Everything had to be well insulated and waterproof. The other responsibility we had was to operate and maintain the system during crossing ceremonies.

The weather was wet but warm. The coastguard crew, with the help of GI volunteers, set up a tank on the aft deck, about 15 feet in diameter by roughly 6 feet deep. It was constructed of a wood frame and a pool liner and filled with salt water with a fire hose. At the edge of the tank was hinged a wood chair, that would flip backwards into the pool. On the morning approaching the equator, after break-fast, the call on the ship's PA system ordered all hands on deck at once. We volunteers were at our stations before the announcement was made.

When the troops and ship personnel, except for those on duty, reported on deck, Neptune Rex's staff was ready for the crossing ceremony. A large tub filled with water, soap suds, and flour was on the ready, as was a two-foot wooden shaving razor. By the way, all the personnel were told on the PA not to have anything on except bare clothing and dog tags. Two good swimmers were stationed in the tank full of water as assistants to Neptune Rex. As for shaving brushes, a large deck-swabbing mop was on the ready. All was on the ready for the ceremony to begin.

At about 10:00 or 11:00 in the morning, the ceremonies began. A crew member dressed as Neptune went along the deck and pointed to one of the soldiers and ordered him to sit on the throne (the wooden chair). Once seated, another soldier would dip the huge deck mop in the soapy slop, rub it on his face, and another fellow with the huge wooden razor would start shaving him as another person would pull the rope that tumbled the chair backward into the pool. This routine was repeated hundreds of times until 2:00 in the afternoon. Since I was on duty manning the PA system I was not part of the dunking. As soon as the ceremonies were over, crews began disassembling the set up, and before dark everything had been cleaned up as if nothing happened. We all were issued our "Shell Back" certificate card as a member of the "Ancient Order of the Deep."

We traveled south along the coast of South America for another day, and then we headed northwest towards New Zealand and Australia. We traveled about two weeks before we passed New Zealand. A few days later we went through the strait of Tasmania, past Sydney, and a week later we docked at Perth, Australia, for refueling and re-supply.

We stayed at Perth two and a half days, and we were allowed to go ashore for the duration. A bunch of us stayed together, and went out to have breakfast and shop for personal things. I went to have breakfast in a diner near the pier where a group of Aussies were eating. When they saw me they greeted me very warmly and asked me what I wanted for breakfast, and I asked them what was good, and one of them said eggs, spam, and chips, and the treat is on us. I had never heard of chips, and one of them told me that it was a special potato, and that while I was in their land I was their guest, and they would order for me. They asked me what I would like for drink, and I told milk. The order was delivered and they told me they would order me a special milk drink. It was. It was a mixture of milk and beer, and one of the Aussies told me it was a popular breakfast drink, and that it was the best thing for my stomach. Some of them had that same drink. I enjoyed that breakfast, and when I offered to pay they wouldn't hear of it. I thought they were the friendliest people I had ever met. The next day a group of us took a train to Fermandle, a 45 minute ride from Perth. It wasn't much of a town, but quaint and we did some shopping. I bought a shaving razor honing stone, which I still have. We returned to Perth by four o'clock, and went directly to the ship.

We departed the next morning for another few weeks before we docked at Bombay, India. In India we were met by heavy monsoon rains. As we got off the ship we were met by a heavy stench, as if something was rotting or raw sewage. We went directly to waiting army trucks, and were carted to a former British base called Worli, located right on the shore of the Indian Ocean. The living quarters were barracks built of solid concrete, which during the rains made them wet and clammy. The food was mostly Australian bully beef and banana fritters, and Indian tea. Next morning we were called to formation, were briefed on our stay at this base for a few weeks,. We were told what not to eat or drink, where not to go, and at what restaurants we could go to eat if we were so inclined to do so. Also we were informed that if any of us were interested to volunteer for standby flight duty we could sign up at the orderly barrack. About half dozen of us signed up. The next day we were notified that we were scheduled for five days of gunnery training. It was not much of a big deal. It comprised of several aerial machine guns mounted on a stone wall facing the ocean and firing on a moving target in the water. We all had to be qualified radio operators to qualify. In the meantime while waiting at Worli we got passes frequently for us to explore the surrounding areas and town. We rented bicycles for less than twenty-five cents an hour. This is how we saw the extreme poverty and misery which was so prevalent in India.

In about two weeks after we arrived in India we got orders to pack our gear, and board a narrow gauge train for Calcutta. The train was comprised of a steam engine and about twenty wooden rail cars. Each car had several four-passenger compartments, and a single low wattage bulb in each compartment. The train was manned by American soldiers. We traveled three full days and nights through jungles, rice patties, and bamboo towns. Isolated stopping stations in the middle of nowhere appeared and we stopped for water and coal or wood for the engine. Local vendors tried to sell us hot tea served in terra cotta cups for two anas (approximately four American cents).

We got in Calcutta in the early afternoon, got off the train, and marched to our billets, old hotels and apartments converted into military quarters. Two to four soldiers in each room made quite comfortable living. In Calcutta the army had a USO, a serviceman canteen, and Red Cross Service center. They had books to read, ping pong tables, playing cards, and phonographs and records to listen to. It also had writing paper for writing letters home. At the Queen Victoria monumental building there was a swimming pool, which we took advantage of and a western dining area where we could have a sandwich, fried eggs, pastries, coffee, and coca cola for a very small price.

After three days we boarded a wide gauge train for Assam. After about eight hours we stopped and transferred to a narrow gauge train. Again all wood rail cars, and manned by American soldiers. About three hours after we transferred into the narrow gauge train several GI's complained to the medics that something had bitten them and had red marks on their skin. They reported this to the commanding officer immediately. In the middle of nowhere and in dense jungles, the commanding officer ordered the train stopped. When we got our clothes and gear at Greensboro, our gear included small DDT- insect killer- canister, so when we were told to get off the train after it stopped, we also were ordered to release one DDT canister in each compartment. Within minutes after we did this, the track and the track bed were completely covered with brown-reddish cockroaches, each 2 ½ to 3 inches in size. It took almost one hour before they disappeared into the jungles, and we boarded the train again. We arrived at the Panduh River crossings before dawn, and since there was no bridge the crossing was accomplished by ferry, four cars at a time. After the train was reassembled, we moved on for a short time and arrived at Kanj Koah; not a real town but a large tea plantation turned into an American and British army camp. Our bashas or bamboo huts were located next to the tea drying shelves and steam curing ovens. The camp was a transient facility and we were there maybe ten days, before moving to Dinjan, a large logistic processing camp and supply airbase. At this base we got everything ready; equipment, transportation, and supplies for operating in Burma (today's Myanmar). We got our on-wheels directional finders, homing stations and support generators and survival supplies. It took two weeks to get everything ready. I traveled alone in a weapon carrier truck, going from repair and supply stations and base station, collecting and delivering electronic equipment to be used in Burma. My only protection was my carbine and side arm. To fool the Japanese operations in the area, the US Army had logistics stations scattered all over the North Assam jungles.

Within two weeks we were ready to roll to Burma by way of the Ledo Road, now called the Stillwel Road, in 6x6 trucks and vans, and jeeps. Me and my partner, Guy Forry, drove a 6x6 van loaded with seven thousand pounds of electronic gear, pulling a trailer with a 5 kw generator, and a jeep. Every two hours we switched vehicles, between the van and the jeep. The trip was a nightmare; steep, muddy road, with rocks and holes and wet all the way. We never traveled faster than five miles per hour, and had to stop every few miles to have our air brakes checked. The trucks had six gears and we had to travel in low-low gear going up and coming down. After days we arrived in Burma and Myitkyna, worn out, dirty, and hungry.

We rested and checked our equipment at the 51st Fighter Control Squadron headquarters located at the edge of the Irrawaddy River in Myitkyna, for approximately one week. As soon as everything was checked out, with the help of the corps of engineers, we drove our station 12 miles into the jungles from Myitkyna. We were located northwest of the city, and that was our workplace and home for 16 months. Aside from going on a mission as a radio operator, we didn't leave the station for 16 months.

The operation of the station comprised of 5 men: 3 radio operator-mechanics, one power equipment operator-mechanic, and one recording and logistics clerk. If one of the operators was missing, the other two would pull 12 hours shifts instead of the 8 hours shifts. If we had time to spare we would write letters back home, do home work, or shoot rats that would invade our basha or huts. After I got overseas I enrolled in a correspondence college course at Ohio University, thru USAFE (United States Army Field Education). Whenever I had time to spare I would study and do my homework. My commanding officer or his assistant, the adjunct officer, would check and sign it before I would mail it to Ohio University. Several weeks later, sometimes months, I'd get the corrected paper with a grade on it.

Our gourmet meals consisted of 3 K-rations per day, and if we could find wild bananas in the jungle we could eat them as long as there were no breaks in the skin. Once or twice a month the supply plane would drop us quart cans of grapefruit juice. During those 16 months in the jungles we helped hundreds of aircrafts to safety, both cargo planes and combat planes that included bombers and fighters. As a standby radio operator, I also went on several missions both combat and cargo to China. During the monsoons our services were most critical, when visibility was extremely low.

Our station consisted of two SCR-640 transmitters, two SCR-639 receivers, one SCR-522 liaison ground to air and air to ground and air-to-air VHF trans-receiver, control units, and two Hallcrafter multi-frequency receivers. Also we had an SCR-510 Liaison low-frequency transmitter-receiver unit for communicating with other stations, headquarters, and field units. We used one of the Hallcrafter Model 342 receivers to listen to the BBC war news when we were not busy or off duty. The station was operated 24 hours a day, 7 days per week, 365 days per year, on 8 hours rotating shifts. If one operator was out for any reason, the other two would be on 12 hour shifts. From time to time we also had to kill a python and bury it, so that we would not have to smell its stench. They weren't too dangerous, and we would try to scare them back in the jungle, but some of them didn't want to take the hint, so we had to shoot them rather than having them hanging around.

We had in our area, by the station, an Allis Chalmer bulldozer-grader, which we all had to learn how to operate it. We took turns, at the end of the day shift, to clear and grade our area of growth all around. During the monsoons you could watch the vegetation grow in and around the jungle. By the way, we rotated shifts every week. For protection we were issued carbines, Thompson machine guns, and to some of us sidearms. At the end of the war, in August 1945, we had left a box of 45 caliber ammunition, around one thousand rounds. We used it to become expert pistol marksman, using a tin can hanging from a branch of a tree 20 yards away as a target.

All during this time Little Nettie and I kept writing to each other weekly, if not more often when I could get the time. I would receive three or more letters at one time when finally the mail would be delivered, many times dropped from the supply plane. At Christmas 1944 Little Nettie sent me a fruit cake in a tin can, that's how they came, which I finally received in December 1945, rewrapped at least four times by the Army Post office (APO). It still was in great condition, and we shared it with my buddies. Needless to say, we were kept very busy in that jungle station, and that was a blessing; otherwise we would have gone insane.

When the war ended in Europe in the spring of 1945, we were hoping that we would be replaced with new crews, and we could return to civilization. That hope was squashed in July when rumors through the grapevine started coming in that we would be invading Japan and we were to prepare for it. A few weeks later the rumors were confirmed, that in September we would get ready to move. At this time the five of us that manned the directional CNS station got together in the operation hut and came to the conclusion that we would never return home. Morale was pretty low, but we carried on as usual. We decided that we would not write home about our feelings. If we did write, most likely it would be censored out anyway.

On the 15th of July 1945, I wrote a long letter to Little Nettie indicating that there would be a possibility that come September, the USA and its Allies would be preparing to invade Japan. Also, we would not be getting replacements to relieve us, so that we could return to the U.S.A. In this letter for the first time, I told her that I loved her for a long time. I also told her that under the existing circumstances, if she so wished, she could date someone else, even though I loved her very much and always would.

When we heard that the first A-bomb was dropped, through the BBC of course, our spirits jumped up a few notches, but feared that the Japanese might retaliate somehow. That didn't happen, and when the second atom bomb was dropped we got our hope back about getting home.

When VJ Day came and the war was over, I was operating the graveyard shift, midnight to 8:00 AM, and at about 5:00 AM I heard the news on BBC on the Hallcraft 342 receiver. I called headquarters, woke up the officer of the day who grudgingly answered and wanted to know why I woke him up at this hour of the morning. I told him, and immediately woke up the commanding officer, and told me to stay on the radio until the CO (Commanding Officer) got verification from the higher command. The commanding officer came back on the radio, and told me to contact the fighter crafts still flying, tell them to return to base by his orders, but don't tell them why. I woke up the other four colleagues, and told them of the good news. They retreated back to the huts and we didn't see much of them for a few days. It seems that our power operator-mechanic by the name of Frenchie, a Cajun from Louisiana, had made himself a still in his power shack, and had prepared quite a bit of booze, made from bamboo shoots, dandelions, and raisins sent from home. Don't need to say more. During those few days, I ran the station, although there was not much to do, and I was able to write home and Little Nettie, and catch up on my homework. For the next two or three weeks we still operated the station, since flights over the Hump still operated, and some directional finding operation was still needed.

Perhaps at this time I should explain how we lived and survived in the jungle. First of all, we got water by means of a 500 gallon tank mounted on a trailer, with a 2 horsepower air-cooled engine running a water pump to fill it. The corps of engineers had made a path to a shallow part of the Irrawaddy River which we used to get water, all purpose water. At the station we had two 55 gallon fuel drums connected together, and mounted on a bamboo platform about 6 feet above the ground, outside and about 30 feet away from our bashas or huts. We filled these drums by pump from the water tank. Out one of the drums was welded a piece of half-inch diameter pipe with a water valve and spicket. At the end of the spicket we hung a juice tin can with lots of nail holes at the bottom. Hence we had a shower al fresco, for all the mosquitoes and jungle creatures to see.

For drinking water, we drank the same water from the river. Exception was that we would fill our canteens and drop a chlorine tablet in it. As for washing and shaving, we used our helmet as a basin or sink. If the drinking water was brown or filled with sediment, we would strain it through a handkerchief before filling our canteens. By the way, we used our helmet to make coffee also.

In September the chore of dismantling the station began. First we had to take down the 90 foot telescoping pole that held the transmitting antenna, which was held up by 16 guy wires and a 2x2 foot base platform. For five men to do this was a pretty risky task, but after several hours we did it. Then came the dismantling and destruction of all the electronic equipment, since it still was classified secret. We burned it and buried it about four feet deep in the ground. Once we cleared the jungle site we returned to headquarters located at the edge of the Irrawaddy River. There we were put to work clearing the area, burning some equipment and papers, packing all the important records and office equipment, and relaxing at last. Our commanding officer personally walked us to a swimming hole at the edge of the river to go swimming. What a treat that was. We did that a few times more before leaving Burma near the end of October 1945. I think the only detachment that remained in Burma was the Mortuary and Registry outfit. Otherwise we were the last active squadron to leave Burma by trucks via the Ledo Road to Ledo, India. This time the road was gravel and smooth riding. We made the trip to Ledo in less than 12 hours. We stayed one day at Ledo, then on trucks (6x6 trucks) for the trip to Dinjian, Assam. Once at Dinjian, we were assigned to our bashas, then directed to go eat at the mess hall, which was a cafeteria in a large bamboo basha. We still had to use our mess kits, but we ate cooked food instead of k-rations. That night I wrote a long letter home and a very long letter to Little Nettie about the events of the last few weeks. Also was able to do considerable studying and homework on my correspondence course.

We left Dinjian after a few weeks on 6x6 trucks on our way to the States. The first day we must have traveled for about 10-12 hours, then stopped at a military post for the night. Same eating arrangements, and sleeping quarters as Dinjian. Next morning after breakfast we boarded the same truck and in the afternoon we reached our destination, an abandoned airbase at Pierdoba, India, not too far from Calcutta. The base had moved out a few weeks before we got there. And everything had been ransacked including the mess hall and kitchen. We were assigned to concrete barracks built by the British, the only building not ransacked and destroyed. We ate from a field kitchen set up in front of the concrete barracks, using mess kits of course. A shuttle truck ran from the barracks to the town which was a few miles from the outskirts of the base, which consisted of a dozen or so shacks, and maybe two dozen lean-to shops, selling knick-knacks, cheap jewelry and dirty books. I went once to town and that was more than enough. On the air base, which looked abandoned with grass growing on the runway and tax strips between the concrete seams. The only aircrafts standing were a few liaison and rescue light airplanes and one C-54 Cargo/transport aircraft. This was the plane that was to carry us to Karachi, for the trip home as soon as an AP (Army Transport) ship was available. Many times during the several weeks we were alerted to get ready to go, just to be told a few hours later that it was cancelled, because of lack of facilities at Karachi. In the meantime the aircraft fuel facilities at the base were closed for good. Finally, a week or so before Christmas we were alerted that we were going this time. To top the C-54's tanks they brought by truck about 150 5-gallon tin cans full of aviation gasoline, which Indian laborers poured into the wing tanks of the C-54.

Before leaving some of us soldiers had bought cheap, used cameras at the vending shacks for the trip home. As soon as the C-54 was fueled and checked out by the crew chief, we started boarding, our duffle bags and any other personal effects were loaded in the cargo bay. I don't remember how many bucket seats were in the plane, but everyone was on board when the door was closed. We were the last transport plane to leave the abandoned air base where B-29's had taken off to bomb Tokyo. The pilot was very kind to fly us over the Taj Mahal so that those with cameras could take pictures. I have a few of these pictures.

We arrived at Karachi air base late in the afternoon. We were brought to a former British camp located in a desert, with concrete barracks approximately 30 feet apart, and lined up in the sand. The mess hall was around two hundred yards away from the barracks, and a PX and beer garden about five hundred yards away. Whenever we went somewhere we got sand in the boots. Once and sometimes twice a week there would be sandstorms, which blew sand through the smallest cracks and spewed sand all over our clothes and bedding. The best part that happened when I got to Karachi was that I finally received the fruit cake that Little Nettie had sent me for Christmas 1944 on December 20, 1945. It was still in the sealed tin can and was still great. Me and my buddies had a feast.

While stationed at Karachi the Red Cross took a group of us on a tour of Karachi. The Red Cross girl in charge hooked up with one of the officers on the tour, and after we got off the truck we didn't see her again until we got on the truck coming back. I and two of my buddies took a walking tour of the city, took a picture riding a camel and another one with a snake man. We walked to the beach, which was so filthy with human feces, that we just turned around and went to the USO, where we had lunch and stayed there until it was time to return to base. It was an historic city but very dirty. I went to the barrack and wrote home and to Little Nettie about my adventures for the day.

On the 30th of December 1945, we were notified that on Dec. 31, 1945 we would be boarding the S.S. General Callan, an army transport, for the USA and home.I did not sleep the whole night thinking about going home and Little Nettie.

Next morning after breakfast, we were lined up in formation on that blasted sand. The roll call was called, were told to collect our duffle bag and any other gear and report where a whole line of 6x6 trucks were lined up.

I should have mentioned about how we spent Christmas 1945. Christmas Eve, the Red Cross planned a hay ride on a camel driven wagon through the desert between 9 pm and midnight. A bulletin was posted asking anyone wishing to go to sign up on the accompanying sheet. About 25 signed up including me. After dinner we reported at the Red Cross center. Two or three camel driven wagons full of hay or straw were waiting in front of the center, with Indian drivers of course. Before 9:00 pm we all got aboard sitting on the straw and went riding in the desert singing Christmas songs, with a beautiful clear sky above. That was a great gift before we embarked for home. Next day, Christmas Day, was like a Sunday. They had a Catholic Mass outside in the desert. Most of us Catholics had gone to confession and received communion during the mass.

We boarded the trucks and started rolling towards the piers where the S.S. Callan was docked. We got off the trucks, fell in formation and the roll call was again called, and some sort of inspection of our possessions was made. One problem was discovered, we still had our weapons with us; well at least many of us. When we left Burma the quartermaster detachment had already left and we didn't have a place to turn our weapons in, so we carried them wherever we went. We couldn't take them with us, so we asked our commanding officer what to do, and he didn't have an answer. As we approached the loading ramp, we dumped the weapons in the water. However, I kept my sidearm in my musette bag which we carried on our shoulder with personal effects.

Again as we entered the ship there was a desk with a non-commissioned officer and a note pad asking for volunteers to work aboard ship. I put my name down and was told to report on the front deck right after lunch. This time volunteering wouldn't be as hard as when we came overseas. I worked mostly in the ship's store most of the way home, although I worked in the radio room doing repairs under the supervision of a Coast Guard NCO. I also did some type-writer repairs, and then back to the ship's store, stocking and selling with a Coast Guard NCO. One day the Coast Guard NCO asked me if I'd like to sell him a pair of my boots, or if I had side arms that I'd like to sell. Since my pistol was an Army issue I was leery of keeping it. He asked me how much I wanted for the side arm. I told him that since it was a .45 caliber, I would take $45, and the sale was made and I felt relieved.

The food aboard ship was absolutely great. Fresh meat, fresh fruits and vegetables, and most of all fresh baked bread. After 21 months overseas and 19 months in the jungles of North Assam and Burma, this was living. I wrote letters home and to Little Nettie to be mailed as soon as we reached port. We stopped at Singapore to refuel for one day. Passes were issued for anyone who wanted to go ashore for a few hours. I went on the wharf, but when I saw how things looked I returned back to the ship, and took my sights from the upper deck. We made another stop at Honolulu to refuel, but looking at the devastation I made no effort to go anywhere. We finally arrived in Washington on February 1, 1946, in the rain and wind.

We disembarked and were led to waiting army busses, which took us directly to a large camp. I believe it was Fort Lewis in Washington. We were taken directly to barracks, where a medical team was waiting to check us out. After we were checked out we went to lunch, and after we were told to go to the barber, either on base if they were open, or off-base where there were several civilian barbershops. At the base barber shop there was a line a mile long and were told there was 1.5 to 2 hours wait. So a group of us went off base, near the entrance to the camp. They saw us coming, because they charged the soldiers 5 dollars for one dollar civilian haircut. They really showed their appreciation! However we did get a haircut without any waiting.

When I got back to the barrack, we were told by an NCO that we could go to the mess hall at any time we wished to have our dinner. I took a few minutes to rest on my bed, then I walked to a big building that was the mess hall. As I entered I was taken aback, when I looked at the brightly painted walls, tiles on the floor and tablecloths on the tables, real tables. I was told to sit at any one of the many tables in the large room. Not many people were in the mess hall yet since it was fairly early. I sat at a corner table, when a man with a heavy German accent dressed in a white cook uniform came over to ask me what I would like to eat for dinner. He told me that he would bring me a large steak anyway I wanted it cooked, and what else would I like with it. I told him that I would like a small head of raw cabbage, a bunch of raw scallions, and a quart of whole milk. He almost laughed, but he did bring me what I asked, plus a well-done t-bone steak and a small loaf of freshly baked bread. I ate everything, except more than half of the steak. What a joy it was to have fresh vegetables and milk.

Next day we were physically checked out, and were asked a bunch of questions, such as where we lived, with whom we were going to live, did we have a drinking problem, and did we smoke. I guess the reason they asked all these questions was that most of us were seriously underweight. I told the doctor that was checking me out, an army captain, that I did smoke cigarettes and I was forty pounds underweight. He gave me some fatherly talk and said to me, "son, would you like to live?" I said yes, definitely, and he told me to stop cigarettes and instead go to the PX (post exchange) up the hill, buy a can of Prince Albert tobacco with a free pipe, and never touch another cigarette. For 41 years I smoked only the pipe continuously, until March 1987 when I retired and stopped smoking altogether.

On this day, in the afternoon, we were briefed that all those soldier living in the east coast would be flown to Ford Dix, New Jersey, for discharge from the military. Next morning, we were ready, loaded on trucks, to go to the airbase for the trip home, when the first sergeant announced that there was another unit in front of us who had priority to the air transports. We were told we would go to Fort

Dix by the Santa Fe railway, in 40 and 8 rail cars. These cars were former cattle cars, converted to hold 48 bunk beds, two high, and carry 48 troops each. The train was equipped with cooking car and dining facilities, using mess kits, probably for the last time. It took 4 days to get to New Jersey from Seattle, Washington. We spent the time listening to soldiers playing guitars, harmonicas, and ocarinas, and of course playing cards. Watching the scenery was another way of passing time. We got to New Jersey on February 6, 1946 in an unrelenting rain. Processing began early the next morning. First we had a one on one debriefing session with a commissioned officer, then another physical exam and finally to the financial records and severance pay. In addition to my regular pay, I received a check for $984 which said it was for rank adjustment. I asked the clerk who handed me the check what it was all about, he told me that I could delay my departure by at least one more day for me to find out. I told him thanks but I would ask no more questions. I wanted to go home.

As soon as we arrived at Fort Dix, we were allowed to make one telephone call home. I called my father, and when he answered I told him I was in Fort Dix he almost cried with joy. Two days before he had received a telegram from the Department of Defense stating that a transport plane went down in the Rockies and that I was missing en-route. He never received any other information to correct the first telegram.

At Fort Dix the last day before we left for home, we were issued all new clothes, shoes, even socks. A group of GI's and women attached the lame duck ribbon on our OD jacket and overcoat to show the world that we were discharged from the military service. When we left the barracks to go to the army busses which would take the dischargees to the railroad and bus station, a man approached us at the gate and asked if those going to New York would like a car ride to Pennsylvania station for nine dollars. Since it was pouring rain I said yes. Five of us crowded into that old car, and in little over two ours I was buying a ticket for a ride on the Long Island railroad to Baldwin, my home.

March 1943- Technical Command School, Truax Field, Madison, Wisconsin.

January 1943 - Dario Antonuci- Technical command school, Sioux Falls, South Dakota.

1943- Mt. Owens, Mojave Desert- Desert combat training

1943- Tomah, Wisconsin- intelligence school.

1944-1945—Burma.   1945- North central Burma

October 1945- Burma— End of WWII   December 20, 1945- C54 at
                                          Piardoba, India- on way Back
                                          to USA.

1944 - Annette Ventura "Little Nettie-
Photo sent to me in Burma.

1945 - "Little Nettie photo sent
To me in North Central Burma.

1945 - Maria Ventura - "Little Nettie's
Sister's photo sent to me in Burma.

December 31, 1945 The SS General Callan-Brought us
home to Seattle, Wash.-Ft. Lewis, Feb. 6, 1946.

Back Home from the Air Corps and Entering Civilian Life

I arrived in Baldwin around 3 o'clock in the afternoon on February 9, 1946. I got off the train with my duffle bag and I took a bus home, while still pouring a heavy rain. I got home at about 3:30, knocked at the door and my father opened the door with tears in his eyes. We hugged and kissed, and did the same thing with my sister. Then my sister told me about the telegram they had received from the Department of Defense. My father asked me how I felt, and if I wanted anything to eat. Then went into the kitchen and came back with a bottle of whiskey and glasses and we had a drink. Then he took a good look at me with a seven day growth of beard, and needing a haircut, and told me to go to the barber shop and get cleaned up right away, and I did. After eating a delicious home-cooked meal that evening, I got on the telephone and called Little Nettie, and told her I would visit her as soon as I got some civilian clothes next day. I didn't want to go around in a uniform with a lame duck ribbon sewn on it. I am not sure but I believe I came home from the army on a Thursday, February 9, 1946.

The next day I went looking for civilian clothes. First I went to Crawford clothing store in Hempstead by bus. There wasn't much there and I took a bus to Freeport to Irving Men's clothing store. I bought a nice grey pin striped suit for around $30 or $35 and a few shirts and socks. While in the army my shoe size hadn't changed, nor my shirt size. When I went in the army I was 135 pounds, and when I came back I was 129 pounds. So all my clothes and shoes still fit. I believe I went to pick up my suit on Saturday, then I called Little Nettie that I would visit her the next day, Sunday, and that I would be taking a train at around 10 o'clock in the morning, which would arrive in Brooklyn at about 11:15 am.

I arrived at the Nostrand Avenue Station just about 11:15 and when I got out of the train there was Little Nettie waiting for me, more grown-up than when I left her three years before. We went for each other and kissed and hugged right on the platform, while it was pouring rain. This was the first time ever that I really kissed a girl, and Little Nettie was the first and only girl that I had ever kissed, aside from my mother when I was a child and very close relatives. As of this day Little Nettie would be my Little Nettie, my girlfriend. She was wearing a whitish gray goatskin winter coat, a dress suit, and black medium high heel shoes. As I saw her on the train station platform, I was full of excitement and love, but I still didn't tell her that, being afraid that she'd get offended or scared. Many years later she told me that she had felt the same way towards me.

We got off the station holding hands, and walked approximately six blocks to her parents and her house in the rain, to meet her mother and father, and her older sister Maria. After we got off the train station platform, we walked across Atlantic Avenue to Nostrand Avenue in a steady rain. On Nostrand Avenue, her cousin's husband's family owned a produce store, and as we approached it, we stopped holding hands. After passing it, we went back to holding hands, until we approached my Little Nettie's house, where we stopped holding hands. I was met by all with friendliness, cordiality and warmth, as an old friend coming home from the army. I tried to act accordingly, and didn't want to give the impression that I was serious about their daughter. To this day I am not sure if they bought it. I was afraid to ask my girl how she really felt about me, and likewise very fond of her, as I had been for a long time already. In the meantime, we stayed very close friends. The parents invited me to stay for dinner, and we chatted for most of the afternoon. They wanted to know my army life, especially life overseas, asked about my plans for the future, jobs and all that sort of chatter. Her mother had prepared a wonderful Italian dinner, and her father insisted I drink wine with the dinner. After we had coffee and dessert, and time to leave. My girl and her sister insisted to walk me to the station, and as I left we shook hands.

Before leaving India and Burma, I had sent for college applications for when I got back to civilian life. Some applications I had mailed from India. I gave my home address as a return address on all for their answers. When I returned home I must have received no less than 15 answers, all stating that there would be at least a three year wait, before they would accept new day students due to the great demand from servicemen who were discharged between 1944 and the end of 1945. They all, or at least most of them, said they would keep my application on file. A few colleges and universities refused outright to send me an application.

There were no jobs to be had, so I decided to go back to high school for refresher courses in English, advanced math, and physics. In the meantime, I applied to Polytechnic Institute for night college. In the following four or five weeks I made weekly trips to Brooklyn Poly, usually on Saturday, and before I'd go I would call my girl and tell her I'd be in Brooklyn. We managed to see each other either at Brooklyn Poly or at her home with her family, since we were family friends. I usually would bring a box of candy when I went to her house. I studied very hard during the week, and also helped my father as much as I could.

In early April I received a letter of acceptance for night college from Brooklyn Polytechnic Institute, contingent upon passing the entrance examinations and aptitude tests. My Little Nettie was attending Fordham University since 1945, and also working part-time downtown at Dunn and Bradstreet and another company. So when I went to take my entrance exams and other tests, I would call her the night before and we would meet after I finished and she got out of school or work. I wasn't that familiar with either New York or Brooklyn, so she would show me the sights, such as the Prospect Park library, the 42nd street library, the New York museum, and even the Bronx Zoo. We'd chat, go for an ice cream and soda, and steal a kiss or two, when nobody was watching. A few times on weekends she would take me to the Fordham Campus up in the Bronx and meet some of her classmates and friends.

There were no decent permanent jobs to be had for returning servicemen. The government had enacted 52-20 club to help veterans for one year. This basically consisted of registering at the state employment agency every week. If you couldn't find a job then you would receive $20 per week. This would continue for 52 weeks or until you got a permanent job, or any job as a matter of fact. Every week I went to register, and asked the clerk if there were any jobs available. I always got jobs, no matter how menial or dirty they were. Almost all the jobs I got were temporary. I always worked and never collected one penny from the government's 52-20 club. I did everything from operating a punch press, soldering radiator covers, welding and running a lathe. I had never done this work before, but when I was shown how, I did it and learned no matter how menial or insignificant it was. Most of these jobs paid less than $20.00 per week. I did this work while going to school at night, most of the time 4 nights per week and taking an average of 8 to 10 credits per semester, and taking laboratory courses on Saturdays. Sometimes if Little Nettie didn't have school on Saturdays, I would call after lab and we would spend a little time together in the afternoon, either at the library or at her home. These were precious and cherished times. This type of working went on until January 1948.

In 1941 Little Nettie's family bought an old two story house that needed lots of work. Little Nettie's father and sometime friends of his would come down to Baldwin on weekends, or vacation days, and work on that house. By the way the house was located five blocks from my father's. The inside was totally rebuilt and some of the outside also. He finished the first floor and around 1945 he rented it to an uncle of mine and his family, who also came from Brooklyn. They were paesani or countrymen. When I came home from the service in 1946, they were still working on the second floor. So during summers, and warm days of 1946 and 1947, I saw quite a bit of Little Nettie and her family when they would come down for the weekends to work on the house. Even my father helped out when he had some time to spare.

Unfortunately, in May 1947, my Little Nettie lost her sister Maria, due to a sudden heart attack at 24 years of age. She was a lawyer and studied in a law office at Court Street, just around the corner of Brooklyn Polytechnic Institute. On May 6, 1947 at around 5:45 pm, I had gotten off the subway at Fulton Street and was rushing to classes when I met Maria in front of Brooklyn Polytechnic, as she was going for the trolley car that would take her to the Bergin Street and Flatbush Avenue Trolley interchange. She told me that the Dodgers had won that afternoon. She looked very pale and tired, and I asked her if she would like to have a cup of coffee with me at the corner coffee shop. She said no, because she wanted to get home and had a lot to do for the next day. I said goodbye and she climbed in the trolley. The next morning I got a call with a sad voice saying that Maria was very ill. I told my sister, and we got dressed in a hurry and got in the train to Brooklyn. On the train, with my heart in my throat, I told my sister that Maria was dead. My feelings proved to be true. My Little Nettie told us that when Maria changed trolleys, as she entered the Bergin Trolley, she put the nickel into the collection slot and dropped dead on the floor of the trolley. Behind her were a priest and a doctor waiting to drop their nickels into the slot. Across the street was the Bergin Street Police Station. I tried my best to comfort my girl and her family, but nothing I or others did could stop the sadness. I felt I had lost a sister too. It brought my Little Nettie and I closer than we were.

When I was working in the city, I would take the subway to get to school, and many times for no reason at all I would get off at the Chamber St. Station with the hope that Little Nettie was there, and in 9 times out of 10 she would be there waiting. She did not know why and neither did I, but it happened more than a dozen times between 1946 and 1948. She usually would be on her way home from work. We just spent a few precious moments together. Sometimes we'd get off near my school together and as I went to classes, she would take the trolley home.

In early spring 1948, while I was upstate in school, my girl and her family moved to Baldwin, five blocks away from my house.

Because of an overflow of students, Polytechnic Institute of Brooklyn made an agreement with the Associated Colleges of upper New York, that Polytechnic would send students with long courses such as drafting, designing and long lab session to the Associated Colleges and credit them with equivalent ratings and grades as

Brooklyn Polytechnic. When students finished these courses, they would return to Brooklyn Polytechnic and resume the regular night school schedules. I took advantage of this situation, since classes would be full day sessions and would give a better chance for better learning, in shorter time as if I had taken these courses at night. In January 1948 I started my first semester at the Associated Colleges in the Utica, New York facility. A World War II hospital converted into a college. In the summer semester of 1948, I was transferred to the Platttsburg Unit. Again a former Army Air Force hospital located on the shore of Lake Champlain. I was there until June 1949, when I returned back to Brooklyn Polytechnic night school. While upstate at the Associated Colleges, I wrote my girl almost every other day and she did the same, and we missed each other very much. This kept my morale up, and gave me the best reason to persevere and do better work. Although we did visit during holidays, and between semesters. She was also very busy during this time going to Fordham University and working part time.

As soon as I returned from upstate New York, I went looking for a job during the day. In a few days I landed a job with the Triborough Bridge Authority through an agency in Hempstead, Long Island, as an electronic maintenance and repair foreman for all the toll equipment on all the bridges, in the New York and Long Island area. These included the Triborough Bridge, the Hudson Parkway Bridge, the Whitestone Bridge, Jones Beach parkway toll booth, the Atlantic Beach Bridge, the Marine Parkway Bridge, and the Woodhaven Bridge in the Rockaways. I would make my rounds every day, but was on call 24 hours a day, 7 days a week. When I went to school at night, I had to call and leave Brooklyn Polytechnic School number, or if I went away somewhere I had to leave that number where they could reach me. On Christmas Eve in 1949 I was invited to spend the evening with my girl and family at her grandfather's house and in the middle of the dinner I got an emergency call from the Triborough that the snow storm had disabled the toll equipment in all but one lane. I put on my coat and started for the door when my Little Nettie said she wanted to come with me, and we'd return together to her grandfather's. I had to replace a tredle on the roadway in that snow and slush which took me more than one and a half hours, and then return and recalibrate all the electronics for another hour, and my poor girlfriend stayed in my car parked on the plaza next to the toll booth in the terrible cold. When I finished, cold as we were, and soaking wet as I was we drove back to her grandfather's. They were waiting for us with drinks and hot food. That night was the last straw, and I resigned the day after Christmas.

At the beginning of December I had applied for a job at the Polytechnic Research and development lab in Brooklyn (PRD) and the day I resigned the Triborough Bridge job, I called PRD and they told me to go for an interview the next day. I got the job as a junior designer and draftsmen, working and developing new types of microwave power supplies for the Air Force. I reported to work on the day after New Year. This was the break I had been waiting for, a good permanent job that I could depend on and start thinking of marrying my girl. Within three months, around the end of March, I was promoted to designer. The first weekend in April I was invited to my girl's grandfather's for dinner with her family and aunt, who lived in the same building, an old brownstone house. It was a cloudy but warmish day, and after dinner, my girl and I went for a walk in the Fort Greene Park, which was located behind her grandfather's. We walked for a while hand in hand, and then we came upon a park bench, painted green, overlooking the Williamsburg bank and the Long Island Railroad Station. We sat down and after a while nobody was walking down the path, I put my arm around my girl and asked her if it wasn't time that we got married. She looked at me sheepishly and she said yes. We gave each other a hug and kiss and walked back to the house, and told her family. I don't quite remember their reaction, but I think it was positive, because her mother asked when we were going to get the engagement ring.

Early the following week we went to see the husband of my girl's godmother who was a jeweler and picked the engagement ring. It was, and is, a one carat diamond mounted on a platinum ring. I used the $984 that I got when I was discharged from the army in 1946 to buy the ring. We went to pick up the complete ring before April 15, 1950, and we got engaged in front of my girl's family A week later we had an engagement party with many of my girl's relatives and friends. When I told my father that we were going to get married, he said, "Dio vi Benedice." (God Bless both of you). My girl gave me a gold chronograph watch for an engagement present.

Now that we were officially and legally engaged, I could ask my girl to go out to a movie, show, or visit friends and relatives without having to ask her father and/or mother for permission. Also to go to the beach, although we almost always ended going with relatives and friends.

My Little Nettie graduated from Fordham in 1948 with a degree in chemistry, and I was invited to her prom to an exclusive place in New York, and we had a wonderful time dancing and meeting many of her friends and classmates. She worked for International Vitamins as a control chemist in Brooklyn for a while. During these days women were not really accepted in the professional workplaces, so she decided to go for her master in education at Hofstra College, now Hofstra University, in the evening school. She got her master's degree in education in 1949, and began teaching elementary school in East Meadow school district, where she taught for 33 years.

As for transportation in getting around, I always had old cars. When I came out of the service, I re-activated my 1935 Oldsmobile for about one and a half years, until I sold it to a newly married couple who begged me for it. In 1947 cars were very hard to get due to the war, and this fellow desperately needed a car for work. Since I was taking the train to work and school, I figured I could do without a car for a while. When I needed a car later on there would be a bigger supply available. The next car I bought was a 1937 Oldsmobile six cylinder in line engine, and I paid less than $100. After about one year it died. When I returned from upstate New York, and started working for the Triborough Bridge Authority, I bought a 1942 Plymouth for $110, which I had to repair continuously. I never traveled without a tool box. I did almost all the repairs on my cars, both engine and body repairs. I did so until 1990.

While working for the Triborough, on November 27th, 1949, we had a fierce hurricane with winds of 100 miles per hour. When the hurricane started blowing early in the morning, I got an emergency call that the Hudson Bridge toll was out. When I got there the electronic control house was under water and I couldn't do anything to help. In the meantime I got emergency calls from the Whitestone and other bridges. I tried to rush to the Whitestone and found out all the electronics were under water, and water was flooding the bridge plaza. I decided to call it quits and go home, but the bridge captain said I couldn't go because the wind was 100 miles per hour, and the bridge was swinging. I decided to go anyway. When I was about two thirds of the way across, a blast of wind swung the bridge so hard that I was tossed from the fast lane to against the outside railing of the bridge. My car suffered a little on the side, but I kept driving until I was off and into Cross Island Parkway. I turned into the Southern State Parkway until I got to Baldwin. The main street in Baldwin was littered with fallen trees and light poles. When finally I got home around 4 in the afternoon, I found out the power was off and nobody had heat. November is a very cold month in the northeast.

My sister had her first child, about six months old, and another family across the street had two small children, and we were the only house in the neighborhood with an active working fireplace. They came to our house for help. My father walked to the coal and fuel place about four blocks away and bought a burlap sack full of pea coal. I drove to Freeport, about a mile away, to a hardware store that sold sheets of steel, and bought a 3 feet by 6 feet sheet of galvanized steel. With it I made a skirt around the fireplace that acted as a radiator for heat. It worked fairly well, and that night we had three families with three children living in our house, and sleeping on a sofa, two chairs on the floor using blankets as mattresses. I checked with my girl and they had no lights but plenty of heat, since her house was manually heated by a coal burning boiler. Although they had a lot of debris from downed trees. By morning most of the houses had electricity and the cleaning up began. At the bridges the water had receded sufficiently for me to start the needed repairs. Luckily there was a weekend after the storm, which gave me a chance to repair the electronics controlling the toll equipment without missing many classes. So much for this episode.

After our engagement we tried to set a date for our wedding. My girl, being the only child left to her family, the parents wanted to give her the best wedding possible within their means. We were looking at a June wedding to be held in Brooklyn. Reason being that her maternal grandfather was too old and feeble to travel. Of course we had to get a dispensation from our parish in Baldwin for this to happen. The next problem was to find an air-conditioned reception hall within close distance of my girl's grandparents. Then only place that met these requirements was the Granada Hotel in Brooklyn, but was booked up for June. The best time that the hotel could give us was July 7, 1951, and we booked it.

We got the dispensation from St. Christopher Church in Baldwin, and made arrangements to be married in the Church of All Saints in Brooklyn, only a few blocks from the grandfather's residence. With me working during the day and going to school nights, and my girl working as a school teacher, we didn't have much time to visit except for short periods on week-ends and holidays. I still had lots of studying to do, and sometimes I had to help my father, but we still managed to attend a few weddings, go to a few shows, and even go to a movie once in a while.

In early June 1951, my father mentioned that the house needed painting, and that he was going to look for somebody to do it. The outside of the house was asbestos siding and didn't need painting, but the inside was plaster and the paint was badly faded. I told my father that before I got married I would do it on weekends and eve-nings. He said no but I insisted, since I lived in that house also. My father was a great landscape gardener, but he didn't know one end of a paint brush from the other. During those days the paint was all oil based, and painting was done only by brush. Rollers weren't on the market yet. By near the end of June I had finished painting the first floor and started the second floor bedrooms and bath. By July the 6th, the day before our wedding, I had one bedroom more to paint. I had worked all day at PRD in Brooklyn, and after supper I started painting the last bedroom. My father told me not to do it, but I insisted in finishing the job before I got married. I finished the job at 4:00 in the morning, while my father was asleep. It was the day of the wedding, and I had to be in Brooklyn at 8:30 am to get ready for the ceremony at 11:00 am.

On the day of the wedding, July 7, 1951, at the 11:00 am mass, Queen of All Saints in Brooklyn, my girl and her family took a train earlier than my father and I did, at 7:00 am. My father and I took a train at 7:30 AM that arrived at Brooklyn at 8:20. We all met at the grandfather's house, where all the tuxedos had been delivered. It was a three-story brownstone house. My girl's aunt lived on the second story, where the bride and her attendants got dressed. All the men, including the groom and the ushers got dressed on the first floor. The wedding was a two tuxedo affair, tails for the church wedding, and black pants and white jackets for the ceremony at six o'clock in the evening at the Granada Hotel. I had seen my girl the day before the wedding and the next time I saw her was when she walked in the church isle with her father, beautifully dressed as a bride. At the exact time that we were married, the temperature inside the all-marble church was above 80 degrees F, and outside the church it was exactly 100 degrees. For a gift I gave my bride an old cameo on gold brooch, which was and is almost like an antique, and very beautiful.

After the church wedding we went back to my wife's grandparents' house, where we all changed into our regular clothes, and ate lunch. There was plenty to eat; sandwiches of all kinds, beer, wine, soda, and hard liquor for anyone wanting a mixed drink or cocktail. In that hundred degree temperature most stayed in the brownstone house, sat in the yard under a tree, or went for a walk in the Fort Greene Park. My best man had a Cadillac convertible, so he took me and my wife and his wife to Prospect Park and parked at the edge of a small lake in the shade. There was a small breeze, so it wasn't too bad.

By four o'clock in the afternoon, everybody gathered at the grandparents' brownstone house to get prepared and dressed for the evening reception at the Granada Hotel. Two limousines came at about five-thirty to pick up the wedding party for the ride to the hotel, which was about ten minutes away. We arrived at just about six o'clock, and went through the usual wedding protocol and then sat down for drinks and dinner. It was a perfectly run ceremonial procedure. There were about 70 guests from my wife's side and about ten from my side. Then there was the usual first dance, then the groom's dance with new mother-in-law, and bride dances with new father-in-law and of course daddy's little girl dances with her father. Finally the best man does the toast and everyone sits for dinner.

We sat down for dinner with the ushers, best man, and brides-maids and maid of honor, at the raised platform. Dinner was served and as everyone was dining my best man engaged me in conversation, and before I knew my wife said to go meet some of her relatives who had come a long distance for our wedding. Needless to say it was a long time before we returned to the dinner table, which had been cleared away by this time. So no dinner for the groom, but I had coffee and cake. We had hired the band until 10:00 pm, but the long-lost relatives were having such a good time that my father-in-law kept it going for another hour until 11:00 pm. Right after the party was over, the wedding party went back to the grandparent's house to change, before retreating. We had booked a room at the Granada Hotel which was a short trip away by taxi cab, although we had told the relatives that we were staying at the Pennsylvania Hotel in New York, just as a precaution in case they had something in mind. All in all it was a wonderful wedding and a wonderful day to remember the rest of our lives.

The next morning we got up very early, had breakfast, and made for the Pennsylvania railroad station in Manhattan, for a trip to Miami, Florida. We didn't have much money so we planned for an economy honeymoon, by going to Florida by train, then going on a cruise to the Dominican Republic, and on the return to visit some of my wife's relatives in Havana, Cuba.

The trip to Miami by train took about 30 hours and we got to Miami on July 9th in mid-afternoon. After checking in the hotel and resting for a little while, we went out to see the sights before going to dinner. The next morning we went to the pier to board the S.S. St. Domingo Cruise ship for the Dominican Republic. The ship was an old steamship, steel hull, and most of the inside steel-framed and wood. Simple but pretty nice and about 18 thousand tons displacement. They served decent food, but the sea and the weather were somewhat rough and most of the passengers became seasick including my new wife. I held up pretty well and tried to bring food up to the cabin for my wife, but she ate very little. At midmorning we stopped at the island of Nassau, but due to heavy rain we saw little of the island, just the shopping areas near the pier. Our cabin was on the main upper deck, so we had a pretty good view of the island. The next morning we went through the windward passage, and I was the only passenger aboard that went for breakfast.

The next morning we docked at the Dominican Republic, in a beautiful sunny morning with a reception committee at hand. While aboard ship we met two wonderful couples on vacation. One couple was a retired army colonel and his wife, and the other couple was a Miami doctor and his wife. The Colonel and his wife found out that we were on our honeymoon and they sort of adopted us. Wherever we went they hired a taxi, and invited us to go with them like we were their children. After the ship docked and we debarked they asked us to go with them to the city of St. Domingo and we went. They were pretty old and I guess they wanted company. The young doctor and his wife joined us, and even bought drinks for us. I think the drinks were Planter's Punch. The old Colonel knew his way around St. Domingo, and told us to go visit the old cathedral of St. Domingo, where supposedly Christopher Columbus is buried. Here we met with the Bishop of the cathedral, and having been told by other couples that we were newly married, he invited us in the church and gave us his blessing for a long and happy life.

We left the next morning in a nice clear day and headed for Port au Prince, Haiti. We got there the next day before noon, and after debarking we toured their outside markets, and bought some liquor and wood crafts. Then after lunch the colonel and his wife asked us to go with them to see the citadel up in the hills. He also invited the young doctor and his wife to go. He hired a taxi and we went up the mountain. As we traveled we witnessed the extreme poverty that existed. The citadel itself was quite old and interesting. After we returned to the pier we did a little more shopping and then boarded the ship for return to Miami. We arrived at Miami early in the morning, debarked and went to the Miami airport where we took a two engine airline to Havana, Cuba, to visit my wife's relatives. We told the cab driver to take us to the best hotel, and he landed us at the door of Havana's Royal Hotel, a real dump.

We checked in at the hotel, went to our room, and immediately called my wife's relatives. Within about one hour they came, picked us up and took us to their beautiful home in the suburbs of Havana.

We spent the rest of the day there and had dinner with them before they took us back to the hotel.

The next morning we were trying to find a place to have breakfast. The hotel had none, so we went out and saw a place like an open air diner. We ordered some pastry and coffee, and my coffee had a dead fly in it. I complained to the server, he took the cup, removed the fly, and gave it back to me. We took the pastry and left, with the fellow in back of the counter asking if anything was wrong, half Spanish and half English. Luckily at about 10:00 am my wife's relatives came to pick us up and took us to their home to have something good to eat. They wanted to know about their relatives in the USA, and everything about our wedding and us in particular. In the afternoon they took us sightseeing, to the club they belonged and to the famous night spots and casinos. That evening they took us to dinner at one of those casinos, that was frequented by the mayor of New York and many famous people. During those days Battista was the ruler of Cuba, and Havana was the gambling center of the Western hemisphere. If it hadn't been for those relatives, we would have taken the airline back to Miami that same day. We could not have stayed in that dusty and dirty place. The next morning we returned to Miami the same way that we had gone to Havana. We stayed in Miami one more day, and then took the train back to New York. All in all we had a simple but wonderful honeymoon, and my Little Nettie and I got to know each other a little better.

Thirty hours later we were back in New York, and on the way to Baldwin, our home. We were happily welcomed by all, especially by my wife's parents, who had our room so nicely fixed up. For the first three and a half years of our marriage we lived with my wife's parents, in the same house. That is, while we were building our own. My father-in-law had started pouring the foundation while we were on our honeymoon. We had bought a large, one cubic yard mixing pan for mixing all the concrete and mortar that was used in building the house. All work was done by hand mostly by my father-in-law, and myself during the evenings, weekends and holidays. The lot had been bought a year before on a tax sale by my wife's parents, for the sum of $750.

After we got engaged my wife's father decided that he was going to build a house for his daughter since we didn't have the money to buy one. However, we did not have the funds to hire an architect, and needed some help in getting the plans. I had seen an ad in one of the trade magazines that I had gotten at work, that dealt with ready, off-the-shelf house plans. It was the Standard Homes Company, Colorado Building, Washington, DC. I sent them a post card requesting information on their house plans. They sent me four volumes of house pictures and plans, with an accompanying letter that explained the details on how to acquire three sets of blue prints for $20 for any house advertised in the four volumes of plans that they had sent me. We went over those books, house by house with my future wife and her parents, and finally picked a two story, six room, one bath, all brick colonial house called the Boumont.

On the following week-end I got a $20 money order at the post office, wrote a note stating who I was and why we needed the blue prints, and mailed it to Standard Homes Company. The following week I received the blue prints, approximately 26 inches by 24 inches in size, a list of materials and a detailed instructions manual on the construction of a house, which I still have 59 years later.

Upon receiving the blue prints, I took them to the building department in Hempstead for approval. The head of the building department was a Mr. Wood, a former civil engineer, and a customer of my father. When I explained the situation, he told me to leave the blue prints with him, and that he would go over them and then we'd get together and go over them. The following weekend he passed by my father's house and left a message for me to call him and make an appointment to see him, and also bring a list of changes that I and my girl's family wanted to make. We got together with my girl and her parents, and came to a decision that we wanted a second toilet and shower downstairs, without changing the outside dimensions of the house. The following Monday, from work at PRD, I called Mr. Wood and made an appointment to meet with him on the following Friday afternoon. I asked my boss if I could get off work, after explaining the situation, at noon the following Friday and he said it was OK. It had to be Friday, because I had night classes the other four days.

Come Friday and I put the blue prints and everything that came with them in my briefcase before going to work in the morning and left for PRD. I went straight to the building department from work on the Friday afternoon. We met with Mr. Wood and his assistant at about 1:30 in the afternoon, took out the two other sets of blue prints out of my briefcase, and sat down to business. He already had made some changes in red pencil, mostly on the pipe size of the sewer system to meet the local plumbing code. I told him of having a second toilet downstairs with a shower if possible, and he suggested that we could replace a fairly large closet, shown on the blueprint between the kitchen and the living room, with the toilet and shower. Luckily the closet was directly under the upstairs bathroom, which presented no problem with the plumbing layout. He marked this in red pencil on the blue prints and put on his signature under it for approval. Before we parted at about 3:00 pm, he told me to apply for a building permit and a plumbing permit. I took the forms with me but left one set of blue prints, and told them I'd mail the permits forms signed by my future father-in-law. The fee for the building permit was $10 and for the plumbing permit $5. The following week we had the permits, and when my new wife and I went on our honeymoon my father-in-law began the building of our house. With the permits we were given about 20 inspection cards. At each phase of construction when completed, we'd send the appropriate card and the inspector would come to check it out and inspect. If the inspection passed the northwest corner would be marked blue, if it failed it would be marked red and need to call the building department for details. During the four and a half years which took to build the house we received one red mark. When we laid out he first story floor beams, out of the 34 beams there was one which was slightly warped and had a small crack in it. The inspector not only marked the northwest corner red, but also marked the beam. Right away we called the Meadowbrook Lumber Company that had delivered the beam, and they came the next morning bringing a replacement beam and took the defective one. We didn't have the money to buy all the material at once, so we bought it as we went. The house was finished to move into in December 1955, and we moved in on December 20,

1955. The build-yourself permits that we got were for five years, with a possible extension due to extenuating circumstances.

During our living in with my wife's parents it was family. My mother-in-law became the mother that I had lost at the age of 10. We got along very well with my father-in-law, and worked together on the house whenever I had the time and chance. We did quite a bit of concrete work together. I laid the sub flooring and I laid all the oak flooring on the whole house during evenings and weekends with the crudest tools; a crow bar, a hammer, and an eight inch power saw, and thousands of cut nails.

We hired a bricklayer to lay the 24000 plus bricks, and a carpenter for the roof. We did all the framing and all the lathing of all the walls. We hired a plasterer for all the wall finishings and the molding. I did all the electrical wiring and my father-in-law did all the plumbing with black pipe and red brass water lines. We moved in before painting the walls and ceilings, and the reason being that the plaster was not fully cured. After we moved in, in late spring, I started painting the interior of the house on weekends, and had it finished by the fall.

We had our first child, a boy, on December 25, 1952 at 11:21 in the morning. We called him Richard Angelo. It was one of the happiest and joyous days in our lives. He was three years old when we moved in the new house. We had no furniture or rugs in the house, with the exception of a kitchen set, a folding aluminum dining room table, and a bedroom set. To entertain the baby, we went to a Vega discount store in Lynbrook and bought a cheap Sylvania TV set, which I got a 10% discount because I was then a Sylvania Electric employee. I took two 4 foot lengths of 300 ohm antenna wire, spliced it into a V, taped it to the wall, and made an antenna for the TV laying on the floor. We watched the cartoons sitting on the floor, and a cold floor at that.

While the house was being built, living with my wife's parents went along quite well, but a very busy schedule. We were four adults living in a five room floor of a two story house, and one bathroom. My father –in-law, myself, and my wife all had to go to work early in the morning. My father-in-law and myself had to leave the house by 6:00 in the morning, and my wife went to work at 7:00. I would get up at 5:00 am, shave and get ready for work, as did my father-in-law. My wife and mother-in-law would follow. We would always have breakfast and coffee before we left.

During the days I had school I would get home between 11:00 pm and midnight, which would happen three to four nights a week. All the times my wife would be waiting with my dinner when I came home from school. Most week-ends were spent doing repairs around the house, or on my car, which needed repairs continually, including changing the oil and lubrication. And of course what little time I had left I studied for school. We were forever tired. On weekends of course, mostly on Sunday, I tried to help in building the house.

Our son was born on Christmas morning 1952, which was a joyous day in more than one way. I took my wife to the hospital Christmas Eve at zero temperature in a 1939 Buick sedan which I had put together from two junked cars. I had bought the cars for $50, one had a good engine, the other a good body. I switched engines, put the good engine in the good body, and vice versa, then sold the bad one back to the junk yard for $35 for scrap iron, after retaining the front axle and wheels for the purpose of making a trailer. After all this was done, I did a motor job on the good engine. Replaced rings, valves, shims on the crankshaft, new spark plugs and points, and rebuild the carburetor. The whole motor job kit cost less than $40. Did the motor job in one weekend all alone. We had that car for over four years, with hardly any repairs needed during this time. With that front axle and wheels that I kept, I built a four foot by eight foot trailer, which we used to go to the market in Brooklyn to buy grapes for making wine, and other supplies. Also used to carry supplies for building the house.

In the spring of 1952 I had a math professor, an adjunct professor, that worked for the Sylvania Research and Development Labs in Kew Gardens, Queens, New York. We got to talk about work, and before the final exams he asked me if I would like to go to work for the Sylvania Research Labs, where he would be my boss. He gave me a brief overview of the work, working conditions, benefits and possible salary. I explained to him that I was working on a classified project for the Air Force and I might not be able to leave my present job until completion of the project. He implied that he would wait, suggested that I discuss this with my present employer. The next day during lunch hour I approached my boss and I brought up the subject. He told me that he would not hold me back as long as I was improving myself, but also implied that he expected me to finish the project that I was working on, which would take me about two more weeks. On the day of my final math exam I told the professor my situation, and he said it was fine with him. He also told me to go see the personnel manager at Sylvania and fill up some papers before I reported for work. The following day I asked my supervisor at PRD for an extra hour for lunch, and I went to see a Virginia Heney, the personnel manager at Sylvania Labs in Kew Gardens. She made me fill up papers for security clearance and told me to fill up my employment application when or after I reported for work. The professor, Lester Feinstein, had briefed her on my qualifications already. I already had security clearance at PRD for Air Force classified work, it was just a matter of having that clearance transferred since the Sylvania research work was also for the Air Force and Navy.

I reported to work at the Sylvania Research Laboratory 2.5 weeks later, and shared an office with my boss, the professor. My first project was to design and produce an improved "mouse trap" for the Air Force and Navy ordinance dropped from the air. The mouse trap is a spring type bomb detonating device, which causes the bombs to explode on contact with another object on the ground. In order to produce such a device I had to design and build the necessary jigs and tools. For this reason I had to learn to operate many machines in the machine shop, such as precision lathes, drill presses, metal forming and cutting machines, metal pressing machines and precision milling machines. Many of these machines I already was familiar with and I knew how to use them. We had all types of materials available to us; both ferrous and non-ferrous. Within about one week I knew how to operate almost all the precision machines in the shop. At the beginning of the second week Virginia Henie, the personnel manager, called me in her office and asked me to fill the employment application, and informed me that my security classification had been transferred from PRD to Sylvania.

In three weeks I had designed the jigs and began to build them. It took more than one week to machine the parts and assemble them, and in another week I had several prototypes of the mouse traps. After doing shock and vibration tests, stress test, and testing on simulation bombs, the design was accepted for production. Once my first project succeeded, I went on to many more such projects, and into the vacuum field. I worked on this type of research until June 1, 1957, when I was transferred to the Sylvania Physics Research Laboratory at Bayside, New York.

I must mention that while I was working at PRD and Sylvania Labs, I was given the incentive that if I received a grade of 90% or above the companies paid 95% of the cost for that course, and if I received a grade of 80 to 90% they paid me back 85% of the cost. It was a great help to me, and other night students.

In college I was majoring in communications and vacuum tube engineering. At the physic lab, the main projects were research in new vacuum tube designs and development, and metal processing using vacuum and hydrogen high temperature processing techniques. For four months I worked as a senior lab technician. After that I was promoted to supervisor of the microwave tube construction laboratory. In this job we constructed tube prototypes, tested and evaluated, and processed same. From a paper design we built and processed in either vacuum or hydrogen furnaces all the parts and components going into the construction of a vacuum tube. We also had started research in growing germanium crystals, developing galeum arsenide doped germanium sensors and devices, and solid state diodes. A major part of the research done at the physics lab was on the development of high power traveling wave tubes and backward oscillators, to be used on counter measure systems on the B58 "Hustler" experimental aircraft for the US Air Force. I loved working in the research labs. I learned more working in the research labs than I would have learned going to school for 50 years.

In the spring of 1959, rumors started going around that GTE was going to take over the Sylvania Research Labs. By summer it was a done fact, and the word got around that the lab was going to move to Mountainview, California. I had graduated from Brooklyn Polytechnic in June, and definitely wasn't going to move to California. I could not leave my father or my wife's parents. I decided to change jobs instead.

Early in August 1959, I sent a few resumes around to people I knew professionally, and in one week I had a few responses. By the end of August 1959, I had accepted an offer from Servo Corporation of America. The Sylvania Labs gave me a farewell fit for a king. An all day affair on the lab lawn, and an Argus 35 mm projector as a gift. I really hated to leave, but under the circumstances I had no choice.

I reported to work at Servo Corp. of America on August 31, 1959, and was assigned the job of setting up a laboratory for assembling and processing infrared germanium sensors for the US Army, and also assigned to be the liaison between Servo Corp. and the army at Fort Monmouth, New Jersey. From the experience at Sylvania I had all the information as to the source of supply for the materials and equipment required for setting the lab up. The complete facility was set up and working in three months. We were assembling, R.F. sealing the sensors, testing and qualifying the product with an 80% to 90% success. When I went to Fort Monmouth and presented the results, the army officials were ready for production and purchase of the units. A physicist at Servo who was in charge of quality control, instead of agreeing with the army, he asked for an extension of the developing contract, so he could perform further evaluation. In other words, Servo Corp. was dragging its feet, and asking for additional development funds, instead of going into production and selling the product. That was enough for me to want out, and I sent my resume to Grumman Engineering Corp. I received a very good offer from Grumman within three weeks, and I took it.

Going back home and to my family. After we moved to the new house, there was a lot more to do. First we had to get some furniture, and maybe some carpeting. The floors get cold in the winter, especially hard oak floors. We talked about it, and decided to let my wife take care of the inside, while I took care of the outside lawn. Landscaping, bush, and flower planting and so on. My father being in the landscaping and nursery business was a great help in planting evergreens and flowering bushes around the house, and along the walk. He gave me some good advice on the lawn also. My wife and her mother went downtown Manhattan to the discount and whole-sale furniture stores and bought a beautiful dining room set. Later on she went back and bought a living room set, and a bedroom set for our little son. Within a few years we had the new house beautifully furnished, and the yard beautifully landscaped. During the summer after we moved in I paved the driveway a little section every evening after work and during the weekends. Also we had several hundred bricks left over, and with them I raised the lawn by eight inches by making an eight inch brick wall on the side and front of the house. This was done over a long period of time in the evening when I didn't have school; a section at a time or piece by piece. My father-in-law and I also did our sidewalk on weekends, piece by piece.

In June 1959 I finally graduated from Brooklyn Polytechnic Institute with a degree in Electrical Engineering, and I was eight credits short for a mechanical engineering degree. Thirteen years of night college's worth. In February before graduation we had our second child; a beautiful baby girl, that we named Rosemary, after my mother Rosa and my wife's sister Maria.

Our second child was like a gift from heaven. After we had our first child we hoped to have more but nothing happened. In the summer of 1957, we made a pilgrimage during my vacation to the Basilica of St. Anne de Beaupire, in Quebec, Canada. The previous year we had bought the first new car in our lives, and in 1957 we drove to Quebec, with our 5-year-old son and my mother-in-law. There were no interstates, highways, or turnpikes during these days, nor were there motels along the way like today. It took us two days of hard driving to Quebec. During the night we stayed in cheap cabins. The new car had a heater and radio, but no air conditioning. Air condition in cars didn't exist during this time. We had a very somber but nice pilgrimage, and the rest of the time we went to see historical sites. While we were in Quebec we stayed in an apartment in a private house owned by a French woman.

In early 1958 my wife went to see a gynecologist to find out why she couldn't get pregnant, and he suggested that she undergo some tests. She did, and after an uncomfortable and painful procedure, she had become pregnant with our second child by June.

Near the end of July 1958, I took my family and my mother-in-law to Miami Beach for a vacation. I took highway US-1 from New York to Maryland, then took US Highway 301 to Florida, then US-1 once more to Miami Beach. It took us 2 and a half days of hard driving (9 to 10 hours per day), but was interesting going through all the towns and cities. Again we stayed in rented cabins for the night. While in Miami Beach we stayed at the Horizon Hotel, less than 150 feet from the ocean beach. My seven year old son and grandmother especially had a good time, as we all did actually.

On the return trip back we took local roads through Georgia, South Carolina and North Carolina. At Ashville, North Carolina we picked up the Blue Ridge Skyway, and rode it all the way to Highway 250 in Virginia. From there we went to Charlottesville and took Highway 29 to Washington, DC, where we picked up US-1 to New York. This was the first time that we had visited the University of Virginia, and as luck and a lot of hard work would have it, my son graduated from this university 15 years later when he was 22 years old. The trip back took us almost four days. Since my wife, my Little Nettie, was pregnant on this trip, my mother-in-law kept warning my wife not to look at alligators since it might affect the baby by old superstitions.

When our new daughter, Rosemary Anne, was born on Friday, February 13, 1959, our seven year old son was ecstatic to have a baby sister. He was his baby sister's constant companion, guardian, and protector, and continued into adulthood. My wife took a leave of absence from teaching school to take care of the baby until the baby was old enough for my mother-in-law to take care of. In the fall semester of 1959 my wife worked as a substitute teacher, and in January 1960, she went back as a full time teacher. She would bring the children to my mother-in-law at 7:00 in the morning and pick them up on her way home at about 4:00 in the afternoon each day.

Although my wife was teaching full time, taking care of the children after she came home, and taking care of the house, she would always have a nice dinner ready when I came home from work and/or school. She never missed a meal, and we always ate together, unless I came home from school late. Until the children went to college we always had our meals together as a family.

After I graduated I enrolled in graduate school at Brooklyn Polytechnic Institute. The graduate school had moved to Farmingdale, New York, only twenty minutes away from my place of work. My company and the school had a cooperative agreement which made life a little easier. If the subjects studied were work-related the company would pay the tuition, plus, on class days, I could leave work one to two hours earlier. I went to evening graduate school for nine years.

On July 11, 1960, I reported to work at Grumman Engineering Corporation, in Bethpage, Long Island, in the position of Electrical Engineer in charge of developing a Primary Electrical Standards Laboratory, and electrical standards and measurement consultant. It was a big order, but within a year and dozens of trips to consult with the National Bureau of Standards in Washington DC, I had a primary Electrical Standards Laboratory and calibration facility operating with traceability to the National Bureau of Standard (NBS). Now that the low frequency laboratory facility was established, I had to begin in getting a high frequency and microwave standards laboratory developed and working within another year, to serve the new line of aircrafts and space programs. This was going to be a multi-aircraft company effort, with the US Navy and US Air Force cooperation and participation. Of course the full cooperation of the NBS would be needed.

On December 12, 1960, while still working on the development of the Primary Electrical Standards Laboratory, I flew to Boulder, Colorado, where the NBS High-frequency microwave standards lab was located, and established liaison contacts between the NBS and Grumman for future cooperative efforts. By June 1961, the establishment of a primary electrical standards and calibration facilities were more or less accomplished, and I began concentrating on the high frequency microwave area of standards and calibration. Advances in aircraft and aerospace technology were being made in a rapid pace, and we were falling behind in the measurement sciences support areas. All the aircraft and aerospace companies were being impacted by these advances, so it was decided that we all work cooperatively to achieve the measurement goals required. Towards this end, on company time, I attended graduate school on the metrology standards fields, sponsored by the NBS at the George Washington University for low frequency, and at the University of Colorado at Boulder for high frequency and microwave metrology. Again sponsored by the NBS.

When I attended George Washington University, I drove down, and after I finished the courses I had my wife and two children fly down by the air shuttle, and had a few days of vacation together. We took the children to the Smithsonian Museum, to the various presidential monuments, to the white house and to see the senate in session. My now eleven year old son commented that he saw Vice President Johnson asleep in his seat, which most likely was true.

Since it was difficult for me to find time for my vacations, several times took working vacations where I combined business and vacation for my family. This was the case when I attended the University of Colorado one summer. The courses were three weeks long, so I arranged with Grumman to drive with my family to Boulder, so that while I was in school, the family could enjoy some vacation. My wife and two children stayed at the Travelodge motel with a very nice swimming pool, I lived in the university dormitory while attending school five days a week. The weekends I spent with the family sightseeing in the Rocky Mountain parks and recreation areas. One week end we drove all the way to the continental divide, and spent time in Estes Park's recreation areas. When going on these kinds of business trips the company would pay me the equivalent airfare for me plus ten dollars. During this time, when gas was cheap, that would pay for all the fuel plus part of the motel charges. During one of the weeks that I was going to Colorado University, we sent our eleven year old son to a western camp run by licensed camp guides, who exposed the boys to outdoor living like the old pioneers did; also were taught crafts and self survival, plus horseback riding. He told us that he loved every bit of the time spent there. We also went on a tour of the National Bureau of Standards, and visited Central City, a replica of the Old West. One day we went gold panning where the two children had a ball, since it was a very hot day.

In my work I was also liaison between my company and the US Navy measuring and calibration facilities in Washington DC and Pomona, California. I also interacted with the US Air Force reference and calibration facilities at the Newark, Ohio Labs. In my work I had to travel a lot between New York and California, Washington, Colorado, and the many other aircraft and aerospace companies. Luckily most of the trips were between two and four days. Once in a while, I had four to six days trips, such as professional planning symposiums, and when I was chairing a National meeting or seminar in the field of metrology. I usually would always rush home early so that I could attend my son's Little League games, especially the weekend games.

In the mid 1960's, I was chairman of a symposium for Grumman Aircraft and General Electric and sponsored by the National Bureau of Standards at Boulder, Colorado, and it turned short of a disaster. The participants, besides Grumman and General Electric, were Boeing Aircraft, North American Aircraft, McDonnell Douglas, Lockheed and a few of the Aircraft engines companies. Grumman made available a G-I Gulfstream to fly the Grumman-GE Team to Boulder. We took off from the Bethpage airfield at 7:00 am, with an estimated time of arrival at Denver at 10:30 am Denver time (12:30 pm Eastern Standard Time). As we entered Nebraska, the starboard (right side) engine started malfunctioning and had to be turned off. We made an emergency landing at Grand Island, Nebraska, a former B-17 Base during the War (WWII), but now a private flying school and general aviation airport. It was pouring rain when we landed. We taxied in front of the one active hangars, a couple of mechanics came out, removed the cowling off the engine, and after inspection they found that the activator in the fuel system was defective. The manager called Lincoln, Nebraska aircraft supply outfit and within less than two hours had flown the new part to Grand Island. Within three hours the engine and the G-1 was ready to continue the trip to Denver. As we entered Colorado airspace a blizzard had started brewing. We landed at Denver airport in a full blizzard in almost zero visibility. Our rental car was still waiting, although we were 3 ½ hours behind schedule. We got to the NBS at 4:30 in the afternoon, and found out that none of the other parties had arrived. The storm continued until next morning, and all the rest of the participants in the symposium had called in that they could not make it. We had a limited symposium with just NBS, Grumman, and G.E.

participation. A total of twelve engineers and scientists. It had taken me almost two months full time in the formation and preparation for this affair. The total participation in this symposium was supposed to have been 125 engineers and scientists, with 15 major aircraft and aerospace companies participating.

At the same time that I was working at Grumman, I had work to do at home. First I had to just about rewire my in-laws' house. It was a 127 year old house, still in use, and the wiring was primitive and all dried out. Used over 600 feet of BX electrical wire to do the job, plus replacing more than one dozen stud and light fixture boxes. Then in 1960 my father-in-law had a stroke whereby he lost all his peripheral sight, and couldn't do any work, aside from a little work in the garden. Since they were living in the second floor of the house, it became evident that going up and down the stairs presented a problem. In 1968, the people next door who owned a 66 year old house passed away, and although the house was in bad condition my in-laws bought it quite cheap. This house was in no way livable so on weekends, evenings, and vacation, I gutted it completely. I rewired it from scratch, redid the plumbing and heating system, and replaced the old slats and plaster walls and ceilings with sheet rock. It had a porch that was part of the entrance, and four windows. Out of the window that was at right angles with the entrance door I made a new door for the first floor. The existing door became the door for the second floor only. Put new lighting throughout the whole house, and brought out all the facilities up to code. Painted the whole house, mostly in the evenings and week-ends. In a little over one year, my father-in-law and mother-in-law moved in the first floor of the house, where my father-in-law would not be in danger of falling down the stairs.

One of the projects that I undertook was the building of a two-car garage at my new house. In 1960, early in the year I started designing an all-brick, hip-roofed, two –car garage to match the house. In less than one month I had the drawings and three sets of blue prints ready to submit to the building department for a building permit. I submitted the prints and discussed the drawings and par-ticulars with the head of the building department and told him that we had built our house ourselves within the last 8 years. He told me that he remembered, and in one week I got the building permit for ten dollars, with the conditions that the building was completed within three years. I completed the garage by 1962. I did all the work manually, including the installing of the two rolling doors. By the end of 1963 I had laid also the ramp and driveway by hand a little section each evening and on weekends. I even put electrical wiring for inside and outside lighting.

In 1965, in the summer I had to participate in an aerospace conference being held at the Disney Hotel in Anaheim, California, and also it seemed that I would not have time to take my family on a vacation during the summer. So I asked my company if I could take my family with me and combine business and vacation. They agreed, and so we took a business-vacation for two weeks. Going to California I took the Old Highway 66, in a new Oldsmobile Jetstar, four door with no air conditioning. I had to be at the conference on Monday morning, so we left around five o'clock Thursday morning, and we got to Anaheim on Sunday afternoon. On the way we stopped to see the Grand Canyon, which my children and my wife enjoyed very much. Before going to Anaheim I stopped at our field office and got three Walt Disney ticket books, for my wife and children. We stayed at the Jolly Roger Motel which was located across Disney World. I reported at the Aerospace Conference at 8:00 in the morning at the Disney Hotel. Proceedings began at 8:30, and I was there for four full days. The conference was attended by approximately 300 attendees, which included engineers and scientists from all over the world, including two scientists from Italy from the Instituto di Alta Frequenza in Milan. While I was at the conference my wife, son, and daughter had a great time at Disney World. The conference over, we started for the trip home. The following morning we started for Yosemite National Park, in southern California. While coming down one of the steep inclines in the park, I felt the brakes acting funny but stopped alright. Later on we had to stop at Idaho Falls and had to have them replaced. In the meantime we continued our trip to Sacramento and to Reno, Nevada. Next day we went to Salt Lake City, Utah, and then to Idaho Falls, Idaho where I stopped at the Oldsmobile dealer to have my Jetstar checked, especially the brakes. When the mechanic had checked the brakes he told me that they had been wrongly installed and that the complete braking system had to be replaced. He told me that everything would be covered under the manufacturer's warranty, and it would take most of one day to do the job. So we had to stay at Idaho Falls for an extra day, which gave me and my family an extra day for sightseeing, which included the huge and beautiful Mormon Tabernacle. Then next morning after the car was repaired, we took off for Montana, North Dakota, and Sioux Falls, South Dakota where I went to Air Force command schools during World War Two. The next morning we headed for Wyoming and the Yellowstone National Park, where the children and wife were thrilled with the geysers, and the bears begging for food. Next morning we headed for Boulder, Colorado to visit old friends and colleagues at the National Bureau of Standards. From there we headed home. I had forgotten to mention that while in South Dakota we went to visit Mount Rushmore; something my children will remember for a long time. From Boulder to New York it took us two long days, driving eleven hours a day, one driver.

Starting in 1961 not only did I have to establish Primary Reference Standards and Calibration Labs for the company, but also had to take in-company courses to keep up with technology advances, and prepare and give talks at seminars related to metrology and measurement sciences, at least once per year. Not to mention taking care of our house, my in-laws' house, and help my father sometimes. I was lucky in some ways to be living five blocks away from my in-laws and two hundred feet away from my father's house.

During the period between 1959 and 1968 I also completed graduate studies in physics and electrophysics, thermodynamics and business management at Brooklyn Polytechnic Institute graduate center in Farmingdale, Long Island. I also embarked in 1963 in taking a correspondence course form the Alexander Hamilton Institute, and graduated by the end of 1964. From 1964 to 1979 I also had taken seven in-company courses.

In 1964 I was principal speaker at the Argonne Nuclear Laboratory in Idaho Falls, Idaho in conjunction with the NBS and the University of Chicago. In 1966 I was chairman of the National Conference of Standard Laboratories, attended by over 1000 engineers and scientists, including the medical profession, from all over the world. At this conference I met and had lunch with Doctor DeBecke, the world famous heart specialist.

In 1976 I took my last college courses in business management given by Cornell University at the Hofstra University Campus. I still took some in-company courses after, to keep up with technology changes.

In 1974 the whole measurement science program including the electrical and microwave primary standards labs and myself were transferred from engineering into the Quality Assurance Department. I was promoted or demoted, depending on how you look at it, to Supervising Senior Engineer of Measuring Assurance and Measurement Standards for the whole company operations.

As chief of measurement sciences from 1962 to 1974, one of the prominent and serious concerns was the way to measure electro-magnetic radiation emanated by the aircraft radars, mainly the APS-95 on the E2C early warning aircraft, which is still in use today in 2009. Until 1962 not much progress was made in this area of mea-surements, although the US Navy and Sandia Corporation in New Mexico had started making studies on the subject. The burden to find a way to measure this parameter was assigned to Measurement Sciences Department. After getting as much of the information avail-able from Sandia Corp, we began experimentation. We started with a steel wool pad soaked in motor oil. With the E2C Radar Full on we approached the radar until the steel wool ignited, then we mea-sured the distance to the radar. We had no idea what the power level was at the ignition point. We knew that the radar output was two megawatts pulse power. We did likewise using photo flash bulbs. We sent the results to the Navy and Sandia Corporation for evalua-tion. These measurements were very crucial to the Navy especially. The E2C aircraft was designed for onboard carrier service, and if too high levels of power were generated it could blow up ammunition aboard the ship. Whatever the power levels turned out to be, they were too unsafe for personnel on the ground. The safe power levels for humans was determined by Sandia Scientists to be 10 milliwatts per square centimeter. I am sure we were being hit with 200 to 500 milliwatts per square centimeter when the flash bulbs popped.

The next mode of RF power measurement was developed by FXR, which consisted of a thermister which converted RF power into heat, and the heat measured on a thermometer dial and calibrated in watts per millimeter equivalent. This unit called a "lollipop" was quite inaccurate, and therefore not too safe. Finally around 1966 or thereabouts PRD developed a densiometer which was fairly reliable and safe to use. In the meanwhile myself and the technicians working for me had gotten blasted with high doses of electromagnetic radiation. Before 1970 we had developed a very reliable means of measuring electromagnetic radiation. The space program and the aircraft industry certainly benefited from these efforts.

In 1965 my wife became pregnant with our third child, Daria. Actually my wife was pregnant during our trip to California, but the doctor thought something else since my wife became very ill, with a pulse rate as high as 200 sometimes. We kept going to the doctor continuously, and finally decided to perform some tests. One of these tests was the radioactive iodine test at which time they discovered that she was pregnant. These tests almost killed my wife and baby. At birth my wife developed uremia and septocemia which almost killed her, and the baby was born with a physical handicap. It was through the efforts of three wonderful and knowledgeable doctors that saved their lives. Doctor Alvin Greenberg saved my wife's life, by staying with my wife in the intensive care night and day for three days. Once I put my two older children to sleep, I rushed to the hospital at 2:00 in the morning, Passover day, and I found Dr. Greenberg trying to make my wife eat a banana in the intensive care unit. Likewise when my little baby was near death Dr. Bronster at 1:00 in the morning rushed in the hospital to perform emergency surgery. He came back to the waiting room one and a half hours later to tell me that the baby would be OK. All this was made possible by the efforts of Dr. Beckman, the head of the hospital, Franklin General Hospital, in Franklin Square, Long Island. Because of the baby's condition we had an emergency Baptism, and I named her Daria. We had a regular church baptism when she was a few months old, and my wife was in better health. For a while it was a trying period for me and my wife, but we made it and Daria grew into a beautiful and successful woman. One of three great joys in our lives. Daria was born March 30, 1966.

In 1965 I was promoted to chief of the measurement sciences section of the engineering department. This imposed the responsibility of budgeting and personnel responsibility, including that of hiring, evaluating, and firing. Also traveling and making speeches at conferences, seminars, and symposiums increased. In 1966, in the spring, I had to chair a National Conference of Standard Laboratories at the Astrodome in Houston, Texas. It took me over six months and lots of overtime to coordinate and plan for the affair. It was attended by over 1000 scientists and technical people from all over the world; approximately 500 from the United States alone.

During this period, 1960 to 1970, we were deeply involved with the design and development of space programs. My department, Measurement Sciences, was responsible for the metrological support of all the ongoing projects. These included the A6A, EA-6b, E2C, F-11, and F14 aircrafts, and the OAO (Orbital Astronautic Observatory) and the LM (Lunar Module) which landed on the moon. On the LM we also did all the testing, qualification, and verification of the search, tracking and landing radars. Of course, throughout my working days, I still took care of our house, lawn, and all that goes with owning a home, including the painting and maintenance. Once in a while I had to pitch in with helping my father and my wife's parents' houses. My plate was always overfull but the love, devotion, and support o f my Little Nettie, my wife, got me through every time.

In 1970, my first born, my son Richard, graduated from high school and entered college, the University of Virginia. He had a very good scholastic record and was readily accepted on early acceptance by the university. This made it easy for the whole family. We had a 1971 Oldsmobile with a huge trunk which did most of the carting of my son's paraphernalia; typewriter, clothing, and all his gear, including a small refrigerator. In the four years that he was in college, that car carried a lot of freight.

In 1974 my whole metrology operation was transferred, including myself, from engineering to the quality assurance department into a new plant. The management was completely changed. I became supervisor of all the electrical and microwave engineering and measurement standards department. Also had the responsibility for calibration procedures writing, review and updating to support the corporate traceability and calibration programs. I remained in this position until 1979. During this time I also did consulting and field problem solving, which took me from New York to White Sands, New Mexico. In my traveling, in many such cases it involved pretty high risks. With my wife's support, love, and devotion, I was able to overcome them all.

In late summer 1979 I was asked to go on a special assignment at the IBM Research Laboratory in Fishkill, New York, for the company. IBM gave Grumman a contract to develop a process for manufacturing an Electronic Beam Lithograph Machine (EBL). The then-secret program contract was named Pocahontas. It was supposed to be a circuit lithograph printing machine which could print up to 4000 circuits on a 30 millimeter by one millimeter thick silicon wafer. Two German scientists had the idea and theory on what this machine could do, but no idea on how to produce or achieve the practical product. Because of my experience, while working in the Sylvania Research Labs, on electron vacuum tubes and electron beam devices, I was one of six people picked for the job. We worked five days a week, sometimes 12 to 18 hours a day. I would drive up to Fishkill on Sunday nights, live in a Holiday Inn hotel for the week, and drive home on Friday nights. Sometimes when we used to work until after midnight on Fridays, I would come home on Saturday morning through that horrible traffic on US 95 and across the Throgs Neck Bridge, or the Whitestone Bridge. On weekends I took care of the house, the yard, and helped my father and my in-laws if need be. It was a horrific pace, but we got the job done and in 1982 we got the production contract from IBM. The EBL machine was produced at the Great River plant; East of Babylon, Long Island. My last effort on this program was writing the assembly manual of the EBL, which consisted well over 550 pages. For this effort I received an Award for Excellence. For the work and effort on the EBL engineering and development, I was promoted to Engineering Specialist (code 0-237-585).

Having completed the special assignment at IBM Fishkill, New York, I returned back to headquarters in Bethpage. The company had received a new renewal contract from the Navy for 59 carrier on board delivery (COD) aircrafts, and had yet not found a support engineer for the job. When I returned from Fishkill, the company offered me the job and I took it.

Before I left the EBL program, on my way to work one morning, I lost sight in my left eye. I became very concerned about it and as soon as I got to my office, I contacted the company medical department. I reported to the medical office and they did a thorough check for a stroke, but instead they found out that I had an extreme cataract of the eye. The medical group gave me a list of eye surgeons that did this procedure, and recommended that I get in touch with one or more of them to take care of my cataract.

Doctor Charles Kelman was doing this procedure by a new technique called Phacomulsification, A technique which extracted the damaged lens through high frequency vibrations and a vacuum suction pump. The vibrations disintegrated the lens into minute pieces, and the vacuum needle, through a very tiny hole on the side of the eye, would suck it out. He was doing this at the Diana Hall hospital in Freeport, a mile away from my home, and so I picked him to do my cataract surgery and implant an artificial lens. I had not thought that this method was still in the experimental stage, so the results were not exactly what I was told it would be. I ended up with a 20/50 vision, but I carried on with my work with one good eye.

As support engineer for the C-2 aircraft, I was responsible for the total aircraft from start to finish. This included the proper construction procedures for the fuselage, electrical systems, mechanical and hydraulic systems, and the complete flight instrumentation and navigation systems. The procedures were written either by Navy or Grumman design and operation departments. My job was to review them, get final Navy approval, and assure that they were properly used and adhered to by all the production departments and personnel.

Spring 1946- Me and little Nettie
In Baldwin,LI, N.Y.

Spring 1946. Me and Little Nettie
In front of her family residence,
46 Rogers Ave.,Brooklyn, N.Y.

Spring 1946- Me and my sister Giulia.

Spring 1946- Me, Litle Nettie
And her sister Maria.

Summer 1946- Little Nettie and
My sister Giulia

Summer 1946- Me and Little
Nettie at Jones Beach,L.I., N.Y.

Summer 1946- Me at Jones Beach.

Winter 1947- Winter Storm,-me
and Little Nettie in front of our
house-- 11 Eastern Blvd.,
Baldwin, L.I.N.Y.

Winter 1947- Me and my sister,- Winter storm.

May 1948- Little Nettie College graduation From Fordham University

May 1948- Me and Little Nettie at her college Prom.

September 1948- Me next to Our flying club's Aeronca Champion plane.

June 1949-Me and Little Nettie at my sister's
Wedding- she was maid of honor.

June 1949- Me in the Aeronca
Preparing for take off—
Platsburg, N.Y. airport.

Spring 1950-Our engagement-
Little Nettie and I.

July 7, 1951 - Our Wedding—
Queen Of All Saints, Brooklyn.

July 7, 1951 - My In-laws-
Mr.&Mrs. Louis and Assunta
Ventura

1956- My father in his nursery
In Baldwin, L.I., N.Y.

June 1959- My graduation from
Brooklyn Politecnic Institute,-
After 13 years of night college.

May 1964 - Chairman;Seminar For the High Frequency
Radio Standards Laboratory, NBS, At Boulder, Colorado.

1964 - Seminar Chairman for The National Bureau of Standards (NBS).

October 1966 - Speaker, IEEE seminar on the technical
Requirements of metrology laboratories

NCSL 1968 - Chairman, Sympsium -
National Conference of Standard Laboratories.

137

October 4, 1975 - My Son Richard's Wedding;
from left- my father Angelo, me and my Son.

October 4, 1975 - Family Photo at My son's wedding.

1975 - Photo of my father Angelo.

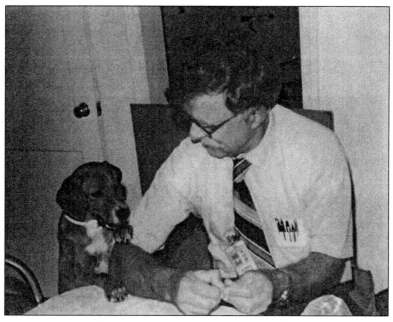

1978 - Me and our beloved Italian Dog Lorenzo

1991 - Our hause that we built In Baldwin, L.I.—
1951-1955: 11 Eastern Blvd., Baldwin

1979 - Me and my father in Driveway of our house in
Baldwin L, I.

1998 - My father's beloved 1956
½ ton Chevrolet pick up truck.
In 1990 brought to Knoxville. T.N.

1990 - My in-law's houses in Baldwin.

My brother-in-law, Frank Ferraro's 80th birthday. From left: Me,
my wife Annette, my sister Giulia, and my brother-in-law Frank.

August 1998 – Reunion of WWII buddies. China, Burma, India Theater, 51st
Fighter Control Squadron, 1944-1945. Reunion held at our house in Knoxville, TN.

Regarding our house, between 1962 and 1966, during weekends, holidays, and evenings, I managed to get the basement finished. I built in a clothes closet, 16 feet of wall cabinets, and book cases, vinyl flooring, wall paneling, and drop ceiling. The cabinets and bookcases were built of ¾ inch finished birch plywood, using only wood pegs and glue. Not a single nail was used. Made a TV and recreation room, and a place for a refrigerator or freezer, and an office for myself. By 1970, I also had replaced the wood window screen and storms, with combination aluminum storm and screens windows.

In 1973 my son and his parents were busy looking at and applying to medical schools. We applied to over 16 medical schools throughout the country, but the responses were slow in coming. When 1974 came and he was ready to graduate from University of Virginia, he applied to CCNY University in New York City for post graduate pre-medical courses and was accepted. In the meanwhile he reapplied to more medical schools. After two semesters at CCNY, no positive answers from medical schools were received so we suggested to my son to apply to foreign medical school. In late spring 1975 we went to the Italian Consulate to inquire about Italian medical schools. They gave him applications and other forms to fill and told him to return them as soon as possible. I also informed the consulate that I was born in Italy and that I still was an Italian citizen according to Italian law. The papers were filled and returned immediately with his scholastic records included. Within a short period we were notified by the Italian Consulate that my son had a place at the Bologna Medical School. If he accepted, he would have to report to Bologna Medical School before November 1975. My son and his fiancée, Mary, had made plans to get married, so the marriage was accelerated to happen before he left for Italy. They were married October 4th, 1975, and left for Bologna about ten days later. During the summer of 1975, my son took a crash course in Italian, and by the time of his wedding he could speak and read the Italian language, well enough to pass the exams. When he arrived at the University of Bologna, they had to find a place to stay, and then attend pre-med school orientations and possibly some testing before starting classes in January 1976. He and Mary spent one semester at Bologna, and then he transferred to the Universita Carreggio, in Florenza, Italy. My son Richard had graduated from the University of Virginia with a very good scholastic background and scholastic record, which was of great help in his undertaking at medical school.

While in Bologna, my son Richard and his wife Mary rescued a mistreated puppy, with two broken legs and a lump on his head. They took him to the veterinary school at Bologna University, whereby they fixed him up. They nursed him back to health, and when my wife and I called him up, he told us that he was sending the puppy to us in the USA. They had called the puppy Lorenzo. Their action towards this dog showed me and my wife the extent of compassion my son and his wife possessed. This has been demonstrated in the decades of medical service he has performed and still is performing as of this day.

About the end of 1977 I asked my son to send me copies of his scholastic records from the Italian medical school, and I would try to fill applications to American medical schools for him to transfer from Italian to American medical schools. He had to go through the Italian consulate to do this, but he managed to do it. As soon as I got his records plus a couple of letters commending his school attendance and performance, I began filling applications which I had previously requested from approximately 12 medical schools. I must mention here that my son worked very hard, and sought every means of getting access to libraries and reference sources to learn, that included getting access to the British Embassy Library. Also in 1977, six months after my father-in-laws' death, in the summer, my wife and our children, and my mother-in-law, went to Florenza, Italy to visit Rich and Mary. I joined them two weeks later carrying two huge suitcases full of medical books and references which we had bought for him. I spent two weeks in Italy. I rented the equivalent of a minivan and took everybody all over southern Italy, and the town and the house where I was born and was raised. Also took them to see and visit the house where my father-in-law was born and raised. I introduced everybody to an old lady, Giovannina, who had given my mother medicine injections and helped taking care of me and my sister when we were little, and my mother was sick.

Rich and Mary returned to the USA in June 1978 for a visit, with intentions of returning to medical school in Florenza for the fall semester. When he told me that he was coming for a visit, I told him to bring with him everything that was important plus all the personal affects, because I had sent more than a dozen applications to medical schools for him to transfer to. As soon as he arrived, when we picked him up at the airport, we found out that Mary was pregnant with her first child, and our first grandchild.

Within a week after they arrived, my son had gotten a job at Meadowbrook County Hospital for the summer as a radiologist assistant. Near the end of August 1978, I happened to be home early and at around 4:00 in the afternoon we received a telephone call from Mt. Sinai Medical School in New York City that they wanted to talk to Richard Antonucci. When we told them that he was working at the county hospital, they asked us to inform him to call Mt. Sinai before 5:00 that afternoon. We immediately got in contact with the radiology department, and the head of the department graciously said that Richard would get the message. My son called right back and we told him to call Mt. Sinai hospital immediately, and he did.

He got an appointment for the next day, and a few days later he heard that he was accepted as a transfer student at Mt. Sinai Medical School. My son later called and wrote to the Italian Medical School and his landlord that he would not be returning to Italy.

In 1976, my older daughter, Rosemary, graduated from high school, and in the fall entered Duke University, in Durham, North Carolina. Most of the girls were lodged at the East Campus of Duke University. The first year she got nice living quarters, but the second year, they moved her to an older building. The quarters that she got were a mess. The walls were all pitted and gouged, the paint was peeling, and the floor was a mess. Just before she was to move in, I took a week of vacation as did my wife, and we went to fix the place. The only assistance from the university was the donation of two gallons of white inside paint. I went to the hardware store and bought what I needed: a tub of spackle compound, putty knives, one trowel, nails, molding and replacement stud boxes for the electrical switches and outlets. I worked from morning to night three full days painting the walls and ceilings. The following years were not as bad. While she was at college she met her future husband, Mark Calvert, a pre-law student.

In 1980 my son Richard graduated from Mt. Sinai Medical School. During his two last years of medical school he was also required to perform medical services in deprived areas of the city and boroughs such as Queens and Brooklyn. It was good practice and made some money at the same time. My little granddaughter Jessica was born, and after living with us for a little while they had gotten an apartment in Bayside to be closer to school and work.

He had applied and sent resumes to several medical centers and hospitals for his internship and residency. After visiting a few of the considered areas, he finally chose Harriman and Anderson Medical Center in Houston, Texas. He had graduated on June 6, 1980 and was supposed to report to the Harriman Medical Center right after Father's Day. They came to live at our house while my son and I did the packing. We rented a U-Haul truck for the moving. We loaded that truck carefully and meticulously, with bedding, medical books, a new television that I had just bought, some other furniture, and children's toys. They already had contacted an agent for an apartment rental, and she would be waiting for us. My son Richard would drive his car loaded with personal effects and books, and I would drive the loaded truck. The wife and daughter would come five days later by air after we had the apartment ready. I took a week's vacation from the special program at IBM, and I had told both my boss at Grumman and at IBM the reason why I was taking the week off. The truck had a governor on the carburetor and we were limited as how fast we could go. We drove 16 to 17 hours per day, to get to Houston in three days. My son was to report to the hospital at 8:00 AM on the 18th of June.

On the third day, June 17, 1980, after 16 hours of non-stop driving, we couldn't drive any further and we stopped at the Century Holiday Inn, in the north part of Houston. We figured next morning in less than one hour we could be at the Harriman Medical Center before 8:00 am. We checked in, and we were told to park the truck in the back of the building. Only passenger cars were allowed in the front and sides of the building, and we were given an inside room for the night. There were two other tucks parked next to our parking spot. We had a double locking bar on the truck, with two heavy padlocks. We locked the truck and went to sleep at around 8:00 pm. We got up next morning at around 6:00 in the morning, and all the trucks were gone, including ours. We went to the desk and they didn't look one bit surprised. We told them to call the police or we would. They did call, and the police arrived in about one half hour. The only thing we heard them say was, "Oh, another one." We called the medical center and they said they understood our problem, and for my son to report to the medical center at his convenience. My son's car wasn't touched, and after we got through with the police we were free to do our business. In the meanwhile the police found the truck empty and stripped on the expressway around the city of Houston.

Luckily I had saved about $2400 from the allowance given to me on the special project at IBM, and was able to buy the necessities and baby furniture for my son's family. I called my company and IBM, and they told me to take as much time as needed to straighten things out. After we finished with all the police reports we rushed to the Harriman Hospital, so my son could get settled in. The staff at the hospital were very understanding and offered any help my son may need. My son's wife and granddaughter arrived five days later to join him. While in Texas my son moonlighted, and went on helicopter medical missions to make some extra money for his family-long hours and hard work is the key to success.

In 1980 my oldest daughter, Rosemary, graduated from Duke University and enrolled in the Master degree program in Zoology. My future son-in-law also graduated from Duke University and enrolled in the law department, working towards a law degree. While studying for a master degree my daughter worked part-time as a professor assistant.

On August 1, 1981 my daughter got married to Mark Calvert at the Renaissance Golf Club, in Roslyn, Long Island. It was a beautiful day and a beautiful wedding. His parents came from Colorado. After the wedding and honeymoon they returned to Duke University to finish up. My daughter got her master degree in June 1982, and my son-in-law got his law degree in June 1983. My daughter also worked on scientific illustrations for medical publications.

In 1983 I was serving as a juror in a criminal case at the state supreme court in Mineola, Long Island, and were in deliberation of the verdict, when all of a sudden my left eye goes dark. I waved at the guard by the door, he came over and I explained to him what happened. He reported to the judge and he came back with the answer that I would not be allowed to leave the chamber until we arrived at a verdict. Leaving before that would be contempt of court and I could be arrested. Luckily we arrived at a unanimous verdict and I was allowed to go to a doctor immediately. It was 4:00 in the afternoon and I called Dr. Kelman who had done my cataract surgery. He told me to get to his office at 58th Street and 2nd Avenue in New York City immediately because it could be a detached retina. I drove to his office with one eye, 20 miles each way, and arrived at his office around 5:00 in the afternoon. He quickly checked and it was a detached retina, and recommended some doctor on Madison Avenue. I said no way, and that I was going to look for someone closer to home. As I was leaving one of his nurses came to me and gave me the name of a retina specialist on Glen Cove Road, Mineola, some six miles from my home. I drove straight home while still daytime, I told my wife everything, and we called the recommended doctor's office. A voice came on and asked if it was an emergency; I said yes and we were told to go to his office at once. My wife drove me there, the doctor examined me right away, and told me that I should have surgery immediately or I could lose my eyesight in that eye. He admitted me to Winthrop Hospital at once and started preparation for surgery early next morning. By far it was a most uncomfortable procedure. For four days I had my eyes bandaged for a total blackout, and had limited head movement. It was an ordeal going to the bathroom for the first two days, but then I learned to go by feel and touch. All total I was in the hospital for about eight days. For about four years after the surgery, I had to wear glasses with a prism in my left eye. I still managed to carry on efficiently with my job for several more years with my good right eye.

In 1981 while my son was doing his residency in Houston, my second granddaughter was born and they called her Laura; a beautiful little girl. My son was working all kinds of hours, and sometimes moonlighting, and my daughter-in-law, Mary, had her hands full with a three-year-old and a baby. Both worked very hard but they managed quite well. We and my mother-in-law went to visit them and tried to help out if we could.

In 1983, my son had completed his residency in Houston, and was accepted at UNC Chapel Hill for oncology and hematology research for three years. I flew down to Houston early in June to help him move. He had rented a U-Haul truck and was partially packed when I got there. We completed the packing, hooked one car to the truck for towing, and the second car the family drove following the truck. I drove the truck and my son drove the car. We had to make frequent stops to take care of the two young children, and once in a while we would switch drivers. It took us, I believe, two and a half days. We arrived at Chapel Hill after dark, and stayed at a motel for the night. My son had made arrangements with a real estate agent about getting a house, and the following morning we all met. The agent had lined a few houses and my son went to see them and chose one of them. It was ready to move in, and the agent arranged for the closing next morning. The following morning we drove to the house and started moving in even before the closing took place. While my son and his wife went for the closing, I stayed with the two little children, and continued to unload the truck and bring its contents into the house. While babysitting I took the girls outside on the deck and porch around the house, and immediately the little one, Laura, almost two years old, was trying to go through the railing of the deck. The 4 ½ year old Jessica was trying to do the same thing. I got them in the house and played until the parents returned. I immediately told my son that the deck and porch railings had to be fixed so the girls would not fall through it. I took their car and went to Sears where I bought a 100 foot roll of vinyl-coated, three foot high wire fence. I returned and fenced the whole railing so that the girls would not fall through it. My son and family spent three years there until he finished his research and went into practice.

All three of our children took piano lessons; some of them grudgingly. Our middle one, Rosemary, excelled in ballet, our baby Daria excelled in music, including piano, violin, and classical singing. Our son excelled in soccer, just like a boy would. We didn't know that Daria could sing, until in 1981 when we went to the Christmas concert at the high school, and she came out on stage and sang "Oh Holy Night." She kept taking singing in high school and through college, and she also took private lessons.

In 1984 Daria graduated from high school and entered Duke University in the fall. At Duke University she pursued singing as an elective subject. During her four years at Duke she sang the Star Spangled Banner, our national anthem, at most of the basketball games. She also performed at several recitals, and at her graduation. Over the last 17 years she has been performing at concerts and amateur opera groups while holding a full-time job during the daytime.

In 1984, near Thanksgiving, my third grandchild, Adrienne, was born to Richard and Mary in Chapel Hill, North Carolina, while my son was doing his cancer research at University of North Carolina. A beautiful little girl. The following year my daughter Rosemary had her first child, Benjamin, another beautiful baby. Also on March 17th, 1985, my mother-in-law passed away after being in intensive care for nine months after she had a stroke. It was very sad for me, because not only was she my wife's mother, but she also was my mother that I had lost when I was 10 years old.

In 1985, just before my mother-in-law died, I had to have cataract surgery on my right eye, and for a while it became quite difficult working on my job. However, after a month or so I managed quite well for a few more years. By this time my job as support engineer for the C-2 aircraft had become routine and had only half dozen aircraft to complete before the contract ended.

On June 1986 my wife retired from teaching after 33 years of dedicated service. She was given a lavish farewell by the school district, her fellow teachers, parents, and the PTA. I was asked to speak on her behalf. What can a teacher's husband say about his wife? I started by saying what a dedicated teacher she was from my daily observations. Also what a devoted mother she was, and what a loving, devoted, and supportive wife she had been for all the years we had been married, and how supportive she was before we were married, in my effort to work full time and get an education at the same time. I don't believe that I could have accomplished what I have without her love and support before and after we got married.

In late fall 1986 the last C-2 aircraft was being completed, and my eyesight had started giving me some problems. I had a few YAG laser procedures, which helped some but still was difficult to do a lot of reading and writing. I submitted my request for retirement on the first of January 1987 for retirement on the 15th. I was called in the office of the director of personnel and asked if I would please stay for three more months and help them to train two engineers to take over my job. I consented to stay until March but no longer, because I was having difficulty with my eyes.

The management assigned two engineers to my program, one had 11 years and the other 8 years with the company, so I figured it would be an easy task to break them in. How wrong I was! I briefed them on the work that entailed to run the program, such as to report at the production plant at 7:30 am every morning, get together with the production personnel and production engineers, go over the day 's schedule, check and approve the production procedures, and check with all the foremen on the equipment conditions and operation. Lastly check on the manpower requirements and availability, and sign off on the schedules and procedures for the day. All this must be done before starting work at 8:00 am. At 8:15 am I would be at my office in Melville, and start reviewing the details and schedule for the next day.

The first week of training only one showed up at the production line by 8:00 am, the other one didn't show up until 8:30 am, and called my office to find out where I was. Getting to the production area at that time, when everyone is busy doing his job, is a worthless effort. This continued the whole first week, and I reported it to management. Also reminded them that come March I would retire. Anyway for the next two and a half months, the situation didn't change much. Once in a while one of the two engineers would show up at 7:30 or 7:45 am. I kept writing a weekly report to engineering management, but things didn't improve much. Came the first of March and I contacted personnel on my retirement, they asked me if I could stay longer, and I told them that my vision wasn't getting any better and that I could not perform my job reliably any longer. They approved my retirement, and I retired on the 20th of March 1987. The company was planning for a lavish retirement party for me, but I told them no thanks, and that if they had I would not be there. Several of my friends were being laid off during this time. Two and one half months later one of the engineers that replaced me called me in a panic, to tell me that they had lost a two million dollar propeller assembly, and what "we" could do. I told him that I retired and had nothing to do with the loss. I also told him that for the five years that I ran the project we didn't have one single mishap, and never lost a penny, and I hung up. The company then called me up, and also sent me a letter, if I would be interested to work as a consultant anywhere from one day to four days a week for them, and that I could choose my own hours. I answered thanks, but no thanks, I am retired.

When I got home at 11:30 am, March 20, 1987, the first thing I did was to throw in the garbage all my pipes, tobacco, and lighters and even the pipe racks. I had been smoking the pipe continuously for 42 years. For one year before that I smoked cigarettes as a necessity to keep awake. It all started in 1944 while I was in Burma. Me and my crew were pulling 12 hour shifts, plus equipment and area maintenance, for a total working shift of 18 hours a day. Although we had plenty of GI coffee to drink, after a while we started dozing on the job. We reported this problem to headquarters, and they sent a special service officer and the squadron doctor to check on us. The conclusion was that there was no additional manpower and we had to cope with the situation. However, the special service officer came up with an unconventional fix. He told us that if we drank strong coffee and smoked a cigarette with it we would stay awake and alert. We tried it and it actually worked. That's when I started smoking cigarettes. Prior to that day I had never smoked and had no intention of smoking. Apparently it became a habit that I couldn't easily get rid of. We used to get two cartons of Pall Mall cigarettes per week. They were dropped by air with our other rations and supplies. When I got back to the United States, I started smoking the pipe on recommendations from the army doctors, and I never stopped smoking until the day I retired from work. I haven't touched one cigarette or pipe since.

In 1985 I had to place my father in a health-related facility. In August 1985 he suffered his fourth congestive heart failure, and was kept in the hospital, South Nassau Community Hospital in Oceanside, Long Island for approximately two months. In October his doctors decided that he needed around the clock nursing care. This was arranged through social services, and on October 15, 1985 he became a resident of Forest Manor Health-Related Facility, in Glen Cove, Long Island. Medicaid was applied for and approved on temporary terms; on condition that his home be put on the market. Upon sale of the house, the proceeds would be used to pay nursing home expenses until depleted. Upon depletion of his resources he would be re-instated on Medicaid. His expenses were met through a special account of the house proceeds, at my company's credit union, which paid 12% interest, in concert with a joint checking account with me, his son.

On November 5, 1987, my father had to be transferred to a full care nursing home, Montclair Nursing Home, at the same location but different building. He received wonderful care, and my family and I would visit almost every day until he passed away. The day before he passed away, we took him for a wheel chair ride outside the nursing home and he smoked one of his cigarettes. He was 91 ½ years old and his lungs were clear. He died January 29, 1989 at approximately 6:00 in the morning, and during the night a storm knocked all kind of debris on the roadways, which made driving very difficult, and we didn't get to him until after 7:30 in the morning.

In 1988 my daughter, Daria, graduated from Duke University with a degree in political sciences. After graduation she went to work for a while and then in 1990 she enrolled at Columbia University for the masters program in International Studies. She did her internship at NATO headquarters in Brussels, Belgium from June to December of 1991, and graduated in January 1992. In 1992 she went to work for the London Times' Office in Washington, DC and from there she has been working in think tanks as a consultant.

When my son started his practices in 1986 in Knoxville, Tennessee, we would come and visit almost once a month, and he would suggest that after retirement we should come and live in Knoxville. We didn't give serious thought to the idea until my father passed away. We had no one left in New York anymore, except my sister and her family. Although when we went to visit my son, for about two years, we would go looking at houses almost every time we came. However, I still had one responsibility left, and that was disposal of my father's nursery.

Although he had transferred title of the land before he became sick, the nursery was his as long as he lived. During the years he was in nursing homes I tried to keep the nursery as clean as possible and take care of the stock on weekends and evenings, and still sold some of the trees and bushes when people called beforehand. I would not ever give a thought of selling it as long as my father was alive. That nursery had been his life. However, by the time he passed away it had become close to a hardship to me. So after his death I tried to dispose as much of the nursery stock as I could by selling as much as I could and giving some away to friends. In the meantime, when we went to visit our son, we started to look at houses more seriously. We found one that we really liked, although it needed quite a bit of work, and in December 1989 we put down a retainer. In February 1990 we put down a deposit, and we closed the deal in early March 1990. We still lived in Long Island, but made frequent trips to Knoxville. While waiting to move we hired a flooring contractor to replace the floor in the hallway, living room and dining room with solid oak flooring. We hired a gardener to take care of the lawn, and my son had the keys to get in and out of the house periodically. Meanwhile we put our house in Baldwin on the market, and tried to liquidate the nursery stock that was left. We took a temporary mortgage while waiting to sell the Baldwin house, which we fully paid in less than one and one-half years.

While still in New York, we tried to get rid of a lot of tools, furniture and other paraphernalia that we did not want to move, plus the two old houses that my in-laws owned. I still had my father's 1956 Chevrolet pickup, but I just couldn't sell it. It was my father's precious possession when he was alive. In the meantime we kept coming to the new house in Knoxville to get it ready to move in. By June 1, 1990 the house in Knoxville was ready to move in. We hired United Van Lines to move us. They sent in a crew to pack everything in the house and also the pickup truck. I had already moved most of my tools, and flower plants and bushes by U-Haul trailer hooked up to my suburban. They drove my father's truck right into the moving van, and then loaded the pickup. We moved to Knoxville June 6, 1990.

As soon as we moved into the new house, in looking over the property (3.75 acres) we discovered a brand new swimming pool under a huge vinyl cover which was covered with leaves and branches of pine and oak trees. When I uncovered it, after removing all the debris, I discovered that all the PVC piping was cracked. Apparently the pool was built the previous summer, tested, but left the water in the pipes, which cracked when it got below freezing during the 1989-1990 winter. I cleaned the pool after removing the cover as best as I could manually and replaced the cover until next spring. I had more important work to do first on the house. For the next three years I spent restoring the house inside and out.

The winter in 1990-1991 was very mild and I was able to work on the house the whole time. In early June I tackled the pool. First I went to Sears and bought 200 feet of 5 foot high chain link fence with two gates, and I had Sears install it around the pool. I also put chain and locks on both gates. Then I replaced all the cracked PVC plumbing with schedule 40 PVC pipe, serviced the heating system, added chemicals and began cleaning the pool. While I was doing

America's Gift to an Immigrant

this my wife went to visit my daughter Daria in Brussels' NATO headquarters. The pool was in perfect shape when my daughter returned from Brussels, Belgium, in late August.

Then I began cleaning the walls and ceiling and painting them. Also rebuilt over the stone wall in the master bedroom. While checking the electrical wiring I found out that it was completely out of the electrical code and dangerously wired. I used close to three 250 feet rolls of 20 AMP. 3 wire romex cable, and more that two dozen stud and switch boxes, to bring the wiring to underwriters' code. The plumbing needed much work which I did, including the flushing system in two of the bathrooms. One of the walls in the master bedroom was bare stone with a stone fireplace. I framed around the stone with 2x4 studs and covered it with sheet rock, to make it look more like a bedroom rather than a mountain. It took me three years to restore that house inside and out. We loved that house and its beautiful view, and my children and grandchildren made good use of the pool in the summer. Many of the bushes and flowers in the garden came from Baldwin, my father's nursery. Brought one of each type and made cuttings down in Knoxville. One of the trees that we brought down from Baldwin was a True Blue Spruce, which we had used for several years as our family Christmas tree. I would dig it up with a large ball of dirt, burlap it, and bring it inside the week before Christmas and then replant it after New Year.

This blue spruce had also other sentimental memories. First, we had gone with my father several years earlier to Princeton Nurseries to buy a flat of these saplings, about 10 inches high for stocking my father's nursery. Second, it had Christmas memories, and third, our Italian dog Lorenzo learned how to lift his leg against it. When in 1992 our beloved dog, Lorenzo, died we buried him, in a vinyl casket, under the blue spruce.

Late in 1993 I started having minor pains in the chest, and we asked our son to recommend a doctor for us to see. He recommended doctor Udit Chaudhuri, which we immediately went to see for a checkup. He did an EKG and some other tests, and gave me some medication to take. The medication helped to relieve some of the pain I went back three months later and did another EKG. This time he put me on Toprol and told me to come back in four months.

Before I went back, in March 1994, my son and daughter-in-law, and my other children, gave me a lavish, super birthday party. It was a total surprise. My son invited me and my wife to a party at his house on the pretense that he wanted his staff to meet me and my wife. When we got there, there were a dozen or more cars parked in front of his house, but it didn't strike a note yet. When we entered a big "happy birthday" was heard. I was 70 years old. Everybody was there; my daughter and family from Raleigh, my daughter from Washington DC, and dozens of friends from Knoxville, plus "Elvis Presley" with flashy suit and guitar.

I went back to the doctor at the end of March 1994, performed another EKG and suggested that I should have a stress test. I had the stress test in April and upon the results he increased the dosage of my medication and told me to watch myself if my pain increased. In the meantime he kept monitoring me. I went right along with working in the yard and monitoring the pool, and doing some painting until the beginning of October, when I began to run out of breath. The doctor performed another stress test, and they sent a copy of the results to my son. The doctor suggested that I go for a catheterization procedure. I said that I didn't want to go through it, but my son and my wife insisted. My son said he'd take me and that he'd be there with me. So it happened; on October 27th at 4:00 pm he took me for the test. I watched on the monitor and what I saw I didn't like. The doctor told me that I should have by-pass surgery, but I told them I wanted to go home and finish what I was doing in my veggie garden, but I heard my son say "Now, Dad." They took me from the test table to prepare me for surgery at 6:00 am next morning. Dr. Maggard performed the surgery, and at Fort Sanders Regional hospital they gave me the VIP suite to recover for five days. Then I was sent home. I cut the lawn on a riding mower the following week.

In 1991 Mary, my daughter-in-law, told me that they needed volunteers at the elementary school, where two of my grand daughters were attending, to run the clinic one or two days a week. I got talked into volunteering and I was "grandfather doc" for five years until after I had open heart surgery. After I had open heart surgery, I started volunteering for the Mended Hearts Volunteers, four years at the UT Medical Center and eight years at the Park West Medical Center.

For years since I was discharged from the army I had been searching for some of my buddies, through military publications and through telephone calls to the various military organizations in Washington DC to no avail. In 1995, in the alumni publication of the University of Virginia appeared an ad for CBI (China, Burma, India) veterans to call the printed telephone number. I called immediately and found out that there existed the China, Burma, India Veterans Association nationwide. I asked for applications and immediately joined. I attended the following reunion in 1995 in Salt Lake City, Utah, and met with several fellow veterans which I hadn't seen for over forty nine years. My wife and I have been attending every reunion every year since.

In 1996 I was complaining of severe stomach pains and also of urinary pains and bleeding. My internist discovered that I had a severe GERD (Reflux) condition and prescribed medication for it. He also referred me to a urologist, who discovered that I had a severe bacterial urinary infection. The urologist put me on a regimen of Floxin for two weeks and then a permanent regimen of Flomax to keep the infection from re-occurring and also to keep my prostrate under control. I also was prescribed medication for chest pains and heart regimen.

In 1997 we received information from the CBIVA (China Burma India Veterans Association) that the Indian and Burmese governments had extended an invitation to US CBI veterans to be guests of their respective countries. The CBI veterans association would handle the details in conjunction with the Indian and Burmese governments. Nineteen veterans and their spouses signed up. We traveled Air India direct to Delhi India, with a refueling stop at London- seventeen hours in the air. We were met at Delhi airport by a very cordial committee and Colonel Singh, our guide. He was a Gurka commander in the Indian Army. He spoke perfect English which made the trip very pleasant. We were given the VIP treatment. We stayed at 4 or 5 star hotels, had great food, an air-conditioned coach, and armed guards in front and back of the coach in jeeps. We were taken to the most historical spots of India, including the

Taj Mahal, Gandhi's memorial and India Gate war Memorial, just to mention a few. The day after we arrived we were given a dinner reception by India's air marshal and other government dignitaries. The air Marshall himself gave me a solid silver miniature replica of a Gurka knife as a remembrance. While at Agra besides visiting the Taj Mahal, we visited the mausoleum of Empress Mumtaz Mahal and the Agra Fort. We also visited several temples, marble and handicrafts shops. In Calcutta we had a bus tour of the city, visited Victoria Memorial, the old courthouse, Hotel Grand and the Kali Temple and gardens.

We left Dum-Dum airport in Calcutta to Chabua airstrip in Northern Assam and then drove by coach to Dibrugarh, central city in Assam. We stayed at the Hotel-East End, and that evening we were given a lavish banquet by the Tea Plantation Club of Northern Assam. We were met by a huge sign which read "Our Heroes."

The next day we visited the railroad center which was operated by American Forces during World War II, visited Chabua which was an air base for American war planes and cargo transports. From Chabua we went to Marguarita Tea Gardens, which during the war had been the 20th Army general hospital for war wounded soldiers and civilians. Now it was a sprawling tea plantation, with nice gardens and buildings. We stayed at the tea garden's luxurious guest house, with gold faucets and door knobs. We had constant servants and valet to serve us whatever we wished at any time. The plantation is owned by the Indian government with a 49% British interest. Before WWII it was owned by the British.

From Marguarita we traveled to Ledo where the Ledo Road, part of the Burma Road, begins. The Ledo Road has been renamed the Stilwell Road after general Joseph "Vinegar Joe" Stilwell, General Commander of the Allied Forces in the Burma Campaign against the Japanese during World War II. Ledo was also where we started the convoy to Burma, where I and my buddy started the long drive with a truckload of electronic gear and a jeep in 1944. We stopped at the Ledo airstrip where a great reception was awaiting us with local music and dancers. It was a great ceremonial affair, even though it was raining. They set up canopies for us to stay away from the rain. Also at Ledo we visited the Allied cemetery, which had overgrown with jungle-like growth but the natives worked all the previous day and night to clear it for us.

From Ledo we went to visit a Kachins tribe village at the invitation of its chief, Prince Bisa Nong Singpho. The village is called Bisa Village, and has no roads, nor electricity or running water and is surrounded by jungles. The Kachins were a great help to us during the war and they didn't forget us. The tribal locals worked for two days with crude, manual tools to pave a path for us to walk on. They even fabricated an arch of jungle trees, vines, and leaves, for us to walk through. There was a small river that we needed to cross, so the natives made a bamboo raft, using two small row boats and lots of bamboo. Because it was raining most o f the time, the natives went and collected river sand and spread it on the path so that we wouldn't slip in the muddy ground. When we arrived the path was lined with hundreds of people and small children and babies. The mothers and fathers wanted their children to touch us and us touching the children as a sign of welcome and friendship. A real touching feeling of affection on both sides. The chief had invited all of us and our guides to have lunch with him at his house, a two level bamboo house, well decorated inside and out. All the buildings in the area were built of bamboo. The house had no chairs but bamboo rugs. We received the food on a banana leaf and ate it with utensils made of bamboo, including the drinking cups. The only means of transportation that we saw were elephants.

We returned to the hotel in Debrugarh, and the next morning we were served breakfast and each veteran and his wife received a gift of Assam tea before we left. Before leaving Debrugah we did some shopping and then left for Jorhat, where there was a reception with local dignitaries and then we had lunch at the Jorhat golf club. After lunch we went by the former camp that I served in 1944, and then to Wildgrass Hotel in Wildgrass- Kaziranga, a real nice hotel. Next morning we got up at 4:00 am to go on a safari at the Kaziranga Wild Game Sanctuary, with the hope of seeing the white rhinoceros. We got to the sanctuary about forty-five minutes later. We were told to go to the elephant loading platform and get on the next elephant. The elephant was harnessed with a saddle with four seats, two on each side. We did that and started on our safari, through tall grasses and bushes as high as the elephant. It was amazing what those elephants can do at the command of its handler. One of the veterans dropped the lens cap of his camera, and at the command of its handler, the elephant picked it up with its trunk and handed it back to its owner in perfect condition.

After we returned from the safari we had breakfast, and then we were taken to an open market shopping tour, with armed soldiers and undercover agents watching for our safety. We returned to our hotel for another dinner reception with entertainment by native dancers.

The following day we set for Guwahati, capital of Assam, at the foot of the Himalayas. We stayed at the Dynasty Hotel, and in the evening a big reception by the governor of Assam. Assam has progressed by far the most since WWII. There are brick and masonry buildings everywhere instead of the bamboo shacks in 1944.

The next day we went to Bagdogra by air from Assam to visit Darjeeling, a rest area during the war, for wounded and regular soldiers. We stayed at the Hotel Sinclaire, and had another big reception dinner. The next morning we were awakened very early for a trip to Tiger Hill at the foot of the big Himalayas, with the hope that we would see the high peaks at sunrise. It didn't happen because of dense fog, but we did get a gift of Darjeeling tea, one of the best teas in the world.

We proceeded to the Park Hotel in Calcutta, where we did some shopping, and attended a fabulous reception dinner given us by the mayor of Calcutta at a fine Chinese restaurant. At this point I had started having trouble with one of my teeth, but looking at the unsanitary conditions in India I hesitated to say anything about it to our guide. The next morning we boarded a Boeing 737 airline for Yangon (Rangoon), Burma. When we arrived at Yangon we were met by a welcome reception with flags and banners welcoming us. In the meantime my tooth was getting worse but couldn't see the swelling yet. After the reception at the airport we boarded an air conditioned coach and headed for Hotel Nawarat, where a sumptuous reception dinner was awaiting us. Before we even started the meal my tooth was killing me with pain, and I told Colonel Singh that I couldn't eat because of the pain. He looked at my swollen face, turned around, and spoke to our host. He made a few calls and within minutes he told me that the premier's personal dentist was going to take care of me. In the meantime the meal was served and my wife was able to eat partially, before two men in native dress came over to take me and my wife to the dentist some 40 minutes away. The two men, presumably undercover police, politely signaled for us to get into the four door Rover for the trip to the dentist. With my devoted wife at my side we followed orders. The Colonel assured us that we were in good hands and that the two men would take good care of us. We arrived at the dentist's office in less than forty minutes, and he was waiting for me at the doorway. He told his nurse to take down my name and prepare the equipment, in perfect English, both he and his nurse. His equipment was around the 1930 era, but in good working order. He looked at my tooth, he told me it was an abscess and it would be taken care of in a few minutes. Without anesthesia he started working on it and within minutes he had taken care of it without any pain. He took two x-rays, put a temporary filling, gave me some antibiotic pills and told me to come back at five o'clock the next day. He went out to give orders to the two men in their native language, and we left for the return trip back to the hotel.

The next day we received an invitation to a banquet given to us by the Burma Minister of Forestry at his mansion at 6:00 pm. I mentioned to our guide, Colonel Singh, that I had to go to the dentist at 5:00 pm, and he assured me that it would be taken care of by the time of the banquet. As planned the two men in native dresses picked me and my wife up at 4:00 pm, took us to the dentist before 5:00, and the dentist had taken care of my tooth by 5:15 pm. The dentist removed the temporary filling, cleaned the wound, repacked it with another temporary filling, gave me two weeks of anti-biotic pills and a copy of the x-ray and we were off to the banquet. What a lavish banquet it was and in the outside gardens.

On the third day our hosts in Yangon took us to visit the famous Taukkyan Memorial Cemetery where British, Burmese, and some American soldiers are entombed. It is beautifully kept, and we (US veterans) were asked to place a wreath with all the ceremonies, in front of the tomb of the unknown soldier. Next we were given a tour of the famous Golden Pagoda (330 feet high), indoor market shopping, great lunch at a Chinese restaurant, and a tour of the lake in a duck boat.

The following day, early in the morning, we boarded a Russian-made Turboprop airplane for Myitkyina where I served for 16 months in thick, dense jungles. It is located in North Central Burma, and during the war was surrounded by high, dense jungles. During the years since the end of WWII the natives took the jungles down and turned the land into lucrative farms, tea plantations, and grazing land for livestock. As soon as we arrived, we were taken by Land Rover vehicles to a luncheon reception at the Hotel Sumpra and a welcome speech by the mayor of the city. We went to visit the former North Airstrip used by fighters, bombers, and cargo aircrafts during the war. We also went to Moungoun, less than one hour away. This city is the ruby capital of the world, and several bitter battles were fought against the Japanese armies. In the evening we were treated to a dinner reception and entertainment by native performers on the banks of the Irrawaddy River. We also were taken to visit the Baptist Mission, the old army campsites, shopping at the Myitkyina market, and indoor shops, and most important of all for me, St. Andrews Cemetery where most American soldiers were buried. When I left Burma in 1945, the cemetery consisted of about five acres of white crosses. When I visited it in 1997, they were all gone; the bodies were transferred either to the states or the national cemetery in the Philippines, and the land turned into farm or residential use. The following day we returned to Yangon by an old, dilapidated German Fokker jet liner, where most the seats and seat belts were broken. The next day we had lunch of Kuchin food at the Puntson Hotel, and then returned to Calcutta to the Park Hotel, and then took a flight to Bombay where we stayed the night at the Hotel Centour. Next morning we left for New York and home.

September, 1998 - reunion at our house in Knoxville, Tennessee of surviving buddies, and their wives, of my squadron, the 51st Fighter Control Squadron, that served in the CBI during 1944 and 1945. We received coverage by all the T.V. and radio stations in Knoxville, and received letters of congratulations and recognition from Knoxville Mayor Ashe, Senator Thompson, Representative

John Duncan and Senator Bill Frist. I have all the T.V. video tapes, and personal videos of the reunion.

Since the reunion in 1998, at least five of the of the 12 buddies have left us to join our Supreme Commander in heaven. One of the highlights of the reunion was that all the wives met with one another. It was a memorable three days for all of us to remember while still in this world, and an eternal memento to take with us when we are called in by our Supreme Commander.

The success of this event could not have been possible without the help of our children: my son Richard and wife Mary, and my daughter Rosemary and son in law Mark.

In 1999, I developed additional stomach pains and going to the doctor it was determined that I had a gall bladder full of stones. They performed surgery the modern way and I had to stay in the hospital only one day. Total recovery took less than one week. A few months later my Little Nettie had to have the same procedure.

In 2000 the CBIVA sent out a bulletin to all its members to inform them that China extended an invitation to all CBI Veterans and families to be guests of the Chinese aviators association in China. They indicated that they would welcome up to 500 guests for the trip, and Air China would supply the transportation at reduced rates. The whole trip would be partially subsidized by the China government. The Hump Pilots Association volunteered to handle the trip arrangements, and 340 veterans and members of their families signed up. It was a very well-coordinated tour.

We departed on Air China from Los Angeles, San Francisco and Detroit to Beijing direct. We departed from Los Angeles and landed in Beijing eleven hours later. When we got to Los Angeles and were waiting to board my wife's name was announced on the PA system to report to the gate attendant. When she did she was informed that our seating was upgraded from business class to first class. We didn't know why, but it was a luxurious ride. After we got seated in first class we were given a drink, a toilet kit, and a pair of slippers. A little later on we were served a five course dinner. The lights were dimmed and we were ready to go to sleep. The trip to Beijing took just about eleven and a half hours. From the airport we were driven to the Sin-Swiss Hotel, a five star hotel.

The next morning we got up very early, had a nice breakfast and left for the airport, where we boarded a Boeing 737 aircraft for Kunming. During WWII Kunming was the main American base for the Flying Tigers fighters, and supply base. The war and other supplies were flown over the Himalayas and carted over the Burma Road to Kunming to supply the Chinese armed forces fighting the Japanese. The change in the city from 1944 to 2000 was like hell to heaven. We stayed at the King World Hotel, a 5 star hotel, with all the modern conveniences, and served western food. Drinking water was about the only inconvenience; we had to drink and brush our teeth with bottled water all through our stay in China. Bottled water was plentiful wherever we went. The next morning we woke up at 5:00 am, ate breakfast at 6:30 AM, and at 8:00 AM the whole 340 of us got together with approximately 50 old Chinese veterans from the China Aviators Association for a group photograph in front of a government building. Right after we boarded air conditioned busses for the Hump Pilots/ CBI Memorial Monument, where formal ceremonies were held with American veterans' participation.

On the 3rd day, we went to visit General Clair Chennault, father and commander of the Flying Tigers, residence, and the famous Horticultural Gardens. In the evening we attended a banquet given by the BAA-KAA organization, where French wine was served.

On the 4th day same routine in the morning, then boarded busses to visit the site of the 14th Air Force base, which is non-existent and has been replaced by vegetable farms. The only reminders still standing are two earth bunkers where airplanes were parked for protection against enemy bombing. From there we proceeded to visit the famous stone forest, and were given a tour of the most interesting sites. Finally we proceeded to colorful Yunnan, an area under development which had a great restaurant, and we enjoyed a great supper. The following day we went to visit the Yunnan Minority Nationality Village, which is like a beautiful park where China's minorities live and carry on business. Some of the best shopping was in this area. While there we had lunch at the South Asia Garden Restaurant.

On the 6th day we woke up at 4:00 am, and boarded busses to airport for nostalgia flight over the Hump and to Shan-gri-la airbase in

Di Quing (pronounced di jhing), located on the outskirts of Lhassa, Tibet. During WWII this was a very secret base where B-29's took off to bomb Tokyo. The other B-29 base was located at Chengdu. The flight wasn't a complete success due to heavy overcast over the Himalayan mountains. We returned to Kunming at about 10:00 am. After lunch at about 2:00 pm we boarded a MD-80 airlines for Chengdu, Sichuan province. We arrived at the Amara Hotel at supper time. Next morning we woke up early and had breakfast early as usual, and boarded busses for Dujiang Dam, an ancient irrigation dam built 2200 years ago and still in full operation, quite a spectacular masterpiece.

Sichuan province is the native area for pandas, and of course we went to visit the pandas in the zoo to watch them eat, sleep on branches and trunks of trees, and just bouncing around. Finally we went to visit the tomb of Wangjian, built in the year 918 AD. Had a great supper, and went to get ready for trip to Xi'an next morning.

On the 8th day, in Xi'an we visited the museum, then went on a tour of the walled city, visited lacquer factory where we bought a beautiful table, visited the terra cotta soldiers and the carriage museum. On the way back we visited the village where General Chiang Kai Shek was arrested just before the war, and then proceeded to a banquet and lavish stage show. Next day we went to visit the Wild Goose Pagoda, oldest existing pagoda and then boarded plane for Beijing.

In Beijing, the next day, had breakfast at 6:30 am, then boarded busses for trip to the Great Wall of China. Made stop at Fresh Water Pearl factory, and saw how pearls are grown and display of pearl jewelry. Arrived at the Great Wall at 12:10 pm; a real marvel to say the least. We left the Great Wall at 2:00 pm for the Friendship Restaurant (government owned), and besides eating we bought some gifts for our granddaughters. At approximately 3:45 pm we left for China's aviation museum which is located in a huge mountain cave. It has all types of Chinese and Russian fighter planes, and also a Flying Tigers P-40 and a Japanese zero fighter.

The 11th and last day before we returned home we were given a tour of the Emperor's summer palace, a very interesting and historical site. We went across the river and lake on a dragon boat. We visited the Cloisonné jewelry factory, where we bought some jewelry. We were given a tour of the Forbidden City, but my Little Nettie and I stayed in the bus, because of the too many steps and long walk. In the late afternoon we were given a bus tour of Tiananmen Square, and in the evening we went to the opera restaurant, where we watched a Chinese opera while having dinner. The next day we left for home. Every day we were treated like VIPs.

In 2002, I had to have another eye surgery, the seventh surgery, on my left eye. This time to remove a tumor, and also re-do the implant. I had to wear glasses with a prism for a while, but it did result in 20/50 vision with the hope that it will improve with time.

One of the happiest times happened in May 24, 2003, when our youngest daughter Daria got married to Dave Moylan. We had a wonderful reception at the Club LeConte restaurant in Knoxville. The church wedding took place in a very old church, the Immaculate Conception Church in Knoxville, that still has a pipe organ. Also my loving wife began to teach me how to play bridge. I learned pretty quickly, but since I am not a lover of card playing, I play under duress most of the times.

In 2004 early in the year I began to get periods of severe pain in the stomach and back, and kept getting worse with passing time. By October the pains kept getting worse, and one day in late October the pains became so excruciating that my loving wife had to drive me to the hospital emergency. The staff was waiting for me when I got there, they carted me to an emergency room and the doctors gave me an intravenous (IV) medication that stopped the pain but almost put my body and mind on fire. My wife said my face was cherry red. After performing a series of tests and calling in a specialist they discovered that I had Crohn's disease and ulcerative colitis. They put me on medication and restricted my diet, and that will continue for the rest of my life. Also they found that my hormone level as just about zero. After recovering somewhat I was discharged from the hospital, and my internist tried to put me on a hormone regimen. That lasted less than two years, when in 2007 my urologist found out that I had prostate cancer. The hormone treatment had to be stopped to prevent the cancer from advancing and spreading. Because of this situation I am always tired, and always shall be.

In 2006 China extended another invitation to CBI veterans and their guests to visit their country. A member of CBIVA volunteered to handle the arrangements. I signed up including my son Richard and his wife Mary, and my youngest daughter Daria and her husband Dave. The arrangements were basically the same as the trip in 2000, except the attendance was much smaller; 16 persons, me being the only CBI veteran. Because of me the whole group benefited and got the VIP treatment. There were, however, a few different events or activities.

The trip started on August 11, 2006, with a scheduled Air China leaving JFK at 4:00 pm. However the flight was delayed two hours. We finally left JFK at 6:12 pm New York time. We stopped at Anchorage, Alaska to refuel. Arrived at Beijing at 11:18 pm Friday August 12 Beijing time. On August 13 we visited China's Aviation Museum in the morning. In the afternoon we were given a tour of the Great Wall of China.

August 14 we took flight from Beijing to Kunming. In the afternoon we went to the International Exposition, where homes from all over the world were shown, besides the beautiful gardens. During the whole tour, which my wife and I had already seen, we sat down by the entrance while our children enjoyed the tour. Directly from the expo we went to feast at one of China's best, if not the best, restaurants in China, the Southern Asia Restaurant. Our children and their spouses had a great time. I was asked to give a speech impromptu, which I did.

On August 15 we went to visit the Hump Fliers/ CBI Monument site, and had to climb the 100 or more steps to the monument. I had the distinct honor to place a wreath at the foot of the monument with the chairman (mayor) of Kunming. The local and national TV and CNN International were there to cover the full ceremony. I was asked to give an impromptu presentation about my activities in Burma and China during 1944 and 1945. This was followed by interviews by television reporters. The whole events were televised during the evening and the next day on local and national TV and CNN International. After lunch we left to visit, by invitation, the Huangpu Military Academy Association in Yunnan Province. We were met by Buddhist personnel, where they escorted us into a Buddhist Chapel, where the monks performed a welcome prayer ritual. Upon completion of the ritual we were led into an oratorium, where I was honored with flowers and gifts. Right after we were entertained by the Oriental Nationalities Art Society. This occurred at Ding Feng Buddhist Temple in San Wa Village.

The following day we went to visit an old nurse (87 years old) who was the head nurse and interpreter at the main allied army hospital in Guilin, China during WWII. Also on August 17, we went to visit, by invitation, the family of China's greatest flying hero during the war. The family still living in a beautiful house are granddaughters, two daughters, and son-in-law. Their beautiful home is in one of China's best closed developments.

On August 18th, we had a tour of the temple of Heaven, which is a marvel of a structure and the beautiful gardens surrounding it. From there we went to attend a huge and lavish banquet, at which time I was asked to make a speech, impromptu of course. Then my son got up and made a wonderful speech that made us, our family, very proud.

Before we departed I was given the most precious and well-appreciated gifts. One of them, a personally made album of the past events in a beautifully made mahogany case beautifully finished, and many other gifts and mementos.

In 2005, in January I began to feel very weak and depressed. We also were thinking of changing houses, because the house on Casa Real Cove, although we loved it more than any house before, was getting to be too much for me to take care of. We had been looking for a house on level ground and with less land to take care of for almost two years, but none of the houses we looked at, new or old, did not meet our needs. Finally in February 2005 a house with one floor living was put on the market in our neighborhood, and we went to look at it. At first we thought it was too big, but after thinking about it we realized it might be just right to meet our needs. We went back, looked at it again and we made an offer. The offer was accepted and in March we closed the deal. By this time I was feeling real bad; weak, out of breath easily, and pains in the back, legs, and chest.

There were many trees around the new house that needed to be cut; seven tall English holly trees right against the wall of the house, three huge flowering cherry trees near the house, and four Bradford pear trees. Feeling bad as I did, I went and cut down all the hollies and one large Bradford pear tree with a chain saw. I just got feeling worse, and decided to go to my internist. After running some tests, he determined that I had both a bacterial and viral infection in my system. For the bacterial infection he gave me an antibiotic, but there was nothing he could give me for the viral infection.

Sick as I was, I continued to clean up the new yard, even though I couldn't sleep nights. The only way I was able to sleep was sitting up in an arm chair. This went on for about two weeks, when I got a little better.

In July we moved, and it was a painful ordeal. I borrowed a trailer, which I hooked up to my suburban and moved all my tools, tractor, some bushes, and a few odds and ends. We hired a moving company to move everything else. Because I wasn't feeling good, we left many things behind, including some beautiful azaleas, and upright evergreens.

I went to the cardiologist where he ran all kinds of tests, including stress tests, catheterization and echogram. In 2006 before summer I got all the results, which indicated that my heart was at 50% capacity. Hence the weakness and aches, but the cardiologist didn't give me anything to take. When I told that to my internist he suspected that the results were not right and ordered new tests, by another cardiologist. The new results showed that my heart function was 37%, and he prescribed me a new medication to help with the pain, and control my blood pressure. With all the other problems, my internist took care of my heart since I refused to go to the regular cardiologist. In 2007 he wanted me to have another stress test but I told him that I wanted to change cardiologist first. I informed my internist of who I would like to be my new cardiologist and he consented. The new cardiologist ran tests in the fall of 2007, including an echogram.

In January 2008 I got the results of the tests, which showed a 35% function of my heart. He put me on a new medication regimen for a period of approximately six months. When he performed another echogram my heart showed an improvement of 10%. Now my heart was functioning at 45% of capacity. In January 2009 the cardiologist ran the same test, and it showed that my heart was still operating at 45% capacity.

In 2008 early in the spring I didn't feel well at all, and didn't feel like doing any work at all. I tried to work a little, then I would go and sit in the porch completely washed out. Many times my wife would come and sit with me, and we started talking about the past. Mostly before and after we got married. We reminisced about our childhood, youth, the war, and everything else. There was nothing left out about my life and my wife's life. It was during this period that I revealed to my wife that I called her Little Nettie from the day I had met her, some 70 years ago, for the first time in the summer of 1939. Although I think I may have called her Little Nettie in some of the letters I wrote to her while in the Army Air Corps.

One of the things my wife revealed was that she felt about me the way I felt about her from our first meeting when she was twelve and I was fifteen years old. At our age, me 85 and she 82, we love each other more than we ever loved each other before. As the saying goes, "Love and friendship is like the shadow of evening, it grows stronger with the sunset of life." Those talks during the spring and summer of 2008 cleared our souls, and we came out with clean plates. We wish we had those talks right after we were married. Our lives would have been richer.

In the meantime, at age 85 years, I still manage to cut the lawn with the help of a tractor, work out the flower beds and do my veggie garden, although smaller than before, and chauffer our youngest grandchild, Samuel, to and from school, piano lessons, and martial arts.

I was handed more than a full plate before and since I became married to my loving and faithful wife. At times I felt that the world was falling on my head. Before I met my Little Nettie, my wife, it was the memory of my mother and the support of my father that kept me going. After I met and married my Little Nettie, it was her love, devotion, support and character that saw me through difficult and trying periods. Without her loving and faithful support I couldn't have made it. God was watching and still is. The love of my devoted and faithful wife has been and still is my guiding light, and it will be until the end.

May 1997 – My wife, Annette *(Little Nettie), and I in front of the Taj Mahal, India. CBI Veterans as guests of India's Air Marshall

May 1997 – My wife Annette and I with Burma's Ministry of Forestry

2002 - Our daughter Rosemary and family:
Mark and Rosemary Calvert, children Danielle,
Benjamin, Emily, and baby Sham

August 2006: Daughter Daria and spouse Dave.

August 2006- China: Me and wife, daughter Daria and spouse
Dave- back row, our son Dr. Richard and spouse Mary.

December 2010- Princess Line Cruise with son's family- left to right granddaughters Jessica and spouse Abe, Laura and spouse Christopher, my wife Little
Nettie- standing; granddaughter Adrianne, son Dr. Richard and spouse Mary.

UP DATE — DARIO
AUTOBIOGRAPHY

Two years have passed since I finished writing my life story, but God has been good to extend my time on earth, and so I am going to publish it for my children and grandchildren. In order to do this right I must bring things up to date.

On October 20, 2007, our oldest granddaughter Jessica Antonucci married Abe Kulkarni in Knoxville, Tennessee. Jessica is a graduate of Tufts University, master degree from Harvard University and a law degree from the University of Tennessee. Her husband Abe is a former captain from the U.S. Air Force and a graduate from the University of Tennessee Law school, and a practicing attorney.

In May 2009 we had another CBI (China, Burma, India Veterans Association) re-union in Aurora, Colorado, and had a great time meeting once more with my WWII buddies, and their wives and children. This I believe would be our 64th re-union since the end of WWII.

Our second oldest grandchild, Laura Antonucci, was married to Christopher Kelly, a lawyer, on December 5, 2009, In Florida; of course my wife and I attended and we had a wonderful time. So good, as a matter of fact, that we decided, my wife and I, to take a 7 day cruise on the SS Westerdam, touring the Caribbean Islands.

In May 2010 we were scheduled to attend possibly the last CBI re-union, but as fate would have it we missed the chance. We were supposed to leave for Reno, Nevada on the 23rd of May, but on the morning of the 22nd I had to rush my beloved wife to the hospital's emergency unit due to a heart mal-function.. She was in the hospital for almost a week with arithmia. This was to be the very last CBI re-union. However, my wife recovered and that is all that matters.

In December 2010 we went on a Princess Line cruise on the SS Crown Princess with our son's family, which included his three daughters and two sons in-law. This took place December 23 to 30. Before and after the cruise we spent a few days at my son's and his wife's ocean front condo in Fort Lauderdale.

We celebrated our birthdays, my wife's 84th on January 20, and my 87th on March 9, 2011.

I still take care of our half acre lawn with the help of a ride-on tractor, our flower beds and my veggie garden. We both drive to do our shopping. Church, taxi our youngest grandchild back and forth to school and music lessons,and drive to the opera and plays in Knoxville.

During our married life and prior to our marriage 60 years ago, we enjoyed the friendship, happy and not so happy days with many lifelong friends. Some are still living and many have gone, but we still maintain the friendship of those living. Just to name a few of those close friends and neighbors:

Annette and Vincent Pascual,Marion and Al Aberle, Elaine and Pierre Preyreigne, Doris and George Gagliardi, Jean and Vincent Tepedino,Elinor and Carl Simpson,Rosalie and Felix Monaco, Miriam and Gene Edelsohn, Tildy and Al Cohen, Anne and Bill Keating, Muriel and Nick Daks, Maia and Harry Quenzer, Warren Seiber, Doris and Jack Calvert, and Connie and Carl Herrgesell.

When I arrived in the USA I was a naïve young farm boy from one of the poorest regions in southern Italy. At my young age I might have known much about nature, such as planting and cultivating, breeding of live stock and caring of animals, but absolutely ignorant of urban life, and progressive and scientific advances and living. AMERICA DID NOT HAND ME A PACKAGE OF WEALTH AND RICHES, BUT HANDED ME THE OPPORTUNITY AND MEANS TO LEARN AND ACHIEVE THE WAY TO SUCCESS, AND TO A HAPPY AND LOVING FAMILY LIFE.

MEMORIES and SUCCESS
Remarks made by Dario Antonucci at
60th Reunion of BHS Class of 1943.

Those people responsible for the fountation of my success in life
in these United States:

**My father - for bringing me and my sister to this country.
Mr. Newton - Superintend of Baldwin High School
Mr. Collister - Principal of BHS
Miss Mary Fuller- Assistant Principal of BHS
All the teachers who went out of their way, and giving of
their time to help a knowledge starved immigrant boy - ME.**

Yes, I got off the boat, the SS Rex, on February 27, 1937, (barely
evading the grip of Benito Mussolini, for I was almost 13 years of
age), in New York harbor. I was enrolled in 4th grade, school No.3
(later became Steele School), knowing not a word of English and
no bi-lingual facilities available, but I made it to the Baldwin High
School in two years. Thanks to the dedication, encouragement and
support of those great and wonderful teachers.

At the BHS I asked Miss Mary Fuller, God Bless Her, if I could
double up in class load. She spoke to Mr. Collister and Mr.Newton,
and they gave me that chance which made it possible for me to fullfil
my high school requirements before I enlisted in the US army Air
Corps on November 20, 1942. Without the encouragement, support
and dedication of the Baldwin High School teaching staff and Mary
Fuller I could not have done it. I still cherish their letters of recommendations and their memories

The cooperation, friendship and understanding of the many BHS
fellow students was a tremendous help. On my part I had to study
long and hard, and missed the extra curricular, the sports, the socials
and others. But it was all worth at the end.

The war took me over through seven US states, Australia, India,
Burma, China, Singapore, Hawaii, and finally in 1946, home.

In trying to get into a day college in 1946, I found out that there were approximately five million other applicants before me on the waiting list. So I did the next best thing and enrolled at night at Brooklyn Polytechnic Institute, studying Electrical and Mechanical Engineering, while working during the day at various jobs until 1949, when finally I was able to get into electrical and microwave research and development fields. I graduated from Brooklyn Polytechnic Institute, and graduate work in Thermodynamics, Electrophysics and Business Management, all at night, while married and raising a family in Baldwin, Long Island, N.Y..

I married my bride, Annette, a school teacher, in July 1951, and my pillar of support. Together we have raised three children: Richard, a physician; Rosemary, B.S. and M.S. in Zoology from Duke University and practicing Scientific Illustrator; and Daria, B.S. from Duke University, Master in foreign affairs from Columbia University, and working as an Arms Control Analyst in Washington, D.C.

We also are grandparents to seven grandchildren. The oldest grandchild, (grand daughter), graduated from Harvard graduate school in 2001; second oldest will be graduating next June from Emory University. The next two oldest will start college at the end of August, 2003. Our fifth will be in junior high; our 6th will be starting high school, and our 4 year old grandson will be starting pre-school in September 2003.

In the meantime, my work as a research engineer and Aerospace Engineering Specialist took me all over the USA. I was metrology section chief on the Lunar Module (LM) vehicle, the F-14, A-6, E-2c, and C-2 aircrafts. Also on the C-2 aircraft I was the power, hydraulic and electrical support engineer before I retired in 1987.

While all this was taking place my family and I managed a few cruises through the Caribbean, several visits to Italy, France, Spain, and the British Iles.

While in retirement we moved to Knoxville, Tennessee, near our children and grandchildren, and managed to visit Canada Northwest, Arizona, Europe Hawaii, Tunisia Greece, turkey and Malta. In March and April of 1997 we visited India and Burma for 20 days as WWII veterans, guests of the respective governments. In April and

May, 2000, we were guests of a Sino-American WWII Veterans reunion in China. Our hosts were the Kunming Aviators Association, The Beijing Aviators Association and China Aviators Association. Three hundred and forty veterans, wives and their children from the USA attended. The occasion being the dedication of a memorial in Kunming - to honor the Hump Pilots, CBI Veterans and the Flying Tiger Pilots and ground crews, that helped China against the Japanese in WWII.

My wife and I are also in volunteer activities. My wife in hospital work, and I a Mended Hearts hospital visitor, and the West Knox Civitan International Club, of which I am a past president - 1997-1998. My wife is very active in Bridge, Newcomers and Welcome Wagon Clubs. Having a home with 4700 square feet of living area, and a four acre yard of which two acres are lawn and flowers and two wooded, keep me quite busy.

We love our new home and adopted state. It's heaven to look out our windows and see Fort Loudon Lake on the Tennessee River looking down, and see the Smokey Mountains looking up.

Yes, it was hard to miss the extra curricular and the socials in high school, but the long hard work was worth the sacrifice. It allowed me and my wife to give this country three professionals, and I hope there will be at least seven more in the near future as a result.

To the youths of today,-this country is full of opportunities. They are there and waiting for you to go after them; don't wait for them to come to you. A person is like a machine: YOU GET OUT OF LIFE WHAT YOU PUT IN, PLUS A FEW HEARTACHES AND DISAPPOINTMENTS ON THE WAY. PERSIST AND YOU WILL SUCCEED.

MEMORIES- UP DATE

Since this account was written in 2003 significant changes in events occurred.

My daughter, Rosemary received a Master degree in education from the University of Tennessee, and is a high school science teacher.

On May 24, 2003 my daughter Daria was married to Dave Moylan at the Immaculate Conception Catholic church, in Knoxville, Tennessee. She is working in Washington, D.C. as a lead organizational development consultant. Dave is a former captain of the US Army, with an MBA degree from Carnegie Mellon University and employed by a global communication company.

My devoted wife and I have managed to spend some time in Tunisia, Scandinavia, Russia, Germany, Portugal, China, Tibet, Las Vegas, 49 of the 50 states, Caribbean Islands, Mexico and Honduras.

Five of our grandchildren have graduated from universities. Our son's and Mary's children: oldest granddaughter, Jessica, BS from Tufts University, MS from Harvard University and law degree from the University of Tennessee. Second oldest, Laura, BS and PHD degree in physical therapy from Emory University and the youngest, Adrienne, BS in architecture degree from the University of Virginia, and studying towards a MBA at the Denver University.

My oldest daughter Rosemary and husband Mark's four children: The oldest, Benjamin, BS degree in English from the University of Tennessee; second oldest, Danielle, degree in Media cinematography, from Northwestern University; third oldest, Emily, junior at Emory University, majoring in political science and Chinese language; and then we have the eleven year old grandson, Samuel, in 6th grade majoring in E-excellence since kindergarten.